KARL
RAHNER

MODERN SPIRITUAL MASTERS
Robert Ellsberg, Series Editor

This series introduces the writing and vision of some of the great spiritual masters of our time. Some of these authors found a wide audience in their lifetimes. In other cases recognition has come long after their deaths. Some are rooted in long-established traditions of spirituality. Others charted new, untested paths. In each case, however, the authors in this series have engaged in a spiritual journey shaped by the influences and concerns of our age. At the dawn of a new millennium this series commends these modern spiritual masters, along with the saints and witnesses of previous centuries, as guides and companions to a new generation of seekers.

Already published:
Dietrich Bonhoeffer (edited by Robert Coles)
Simone Weil (edited by Eric O. Springsted)
Henri Nouwen (edited by Robert A. Jonas)
Pierre Teilhard de Chardin (edited by Ursula King)
Anthony de Mello (edited by William Dych, S.J.)
Charles de Foucauld (edited by Robert Ellsberg)
Oscar Romero (by Marie Dennis, Rennie Golden,
    and Scott Wright)
Eberhard Arnold (edited by Johann Christoph Arnold)
Thomas Merton (edited by Christine M. Bochen)
Thich Nhat Hanh (edited by Robert Ellsberg)
Rufus Jones (edited by Kerry Walters)
Mother Teresa (edited by Jean Maalouf)
Edith Stein (edited by John Sullivan, O.C.D.)
John Main (edited by Laurence Freeman)
Mohandas Gandhi (edited by John Dear)
Mother Maria Skobtsova (introduction by Jim Forest)
Evelyn Underhill (edited by Emilie Griffin)
St. Thérèse of Lisieux (edited by Mary Frohlich)
Flannery O'Connor (edited by Robert Ellsberg)
Clarence Jordan (edited by Joyce Hollyday)
Alfred Delp, SJ (introduction by Thomas Merton)

KARL RAHNER

Spiritual Writings

Edited with an Introduction by
PHILIP ENDEAN

ORBIS BOOKS

Maryknoll, New York 10545

Founded in 1970, Orbis Books endeavors to publish works that enlighten the mind, nourish the spirit, and challenge the conscience. The publishing arm of the Maryknoll Fathers and Brothers, Orbis seeks to explore the global dimensions of the Christian faith and mission, to invite dialogue with diverse cultures and religious traditions, and to serve the cause of reconciliation and peace. The books published reflect the views of their authors and do not represent the official position of the Maryknoll Society. To learn more about Maryknoll and Orbis Books, please visit our website at www.maryknoll.org.

Manufactured in the United States of America.

Library of Congress Cataloging-in-Publication Data

Rahner, Karl, 1904-
    [Selections. English. 2004]
    Spiritual writings / Karl Rahner ; edited with an introduction by Philip Endean.
        p. cm. – (Modern spiritual masters series)
    Includes bibliographical references (p.   ).
    ISBN 1-57075-553-1 (pbk.)
    1. Theology, Doctrinal. I. Endean, Philip, 1954- II. Title. III. Series.
BT75.3.R34 2004
230'.2 – dc22
                                                                    2004008031

Contents

Acknowledgments

This anthology, presenting Rahner in ways that may seem new, owes much to the vision and patience of Robert Ellsberg — thanks to him and to the team at Orbis, especially John Eagleson. I am grateful, too, to Lutz Hoffmann in Munich for facilitating what turned out to be a complicated process of checking copyright permissions; to Gerry Hughes in Oxford for reading a draft of this book carefully and for making many helpful suggestions about the translations; and to Roman Siebenrock in Innsbruck, the Rahner archivist, for many kindnesses, notably for help with transcription of the Stanislaus piece.

PE sj

Introduction

Karl Rahner came to Heythrop College in London in February 1984 for a celebration of his eightieth birthday. Six weeks or so later, he was dead — be the truth told, he had probably overdone the celebrations. The London gathering centered on a guest lecture in his honor by the distinguished Oxford theologian, John Macquarrie,[1] and many notable people were present. Rahner sat on the podium. He did not understand English well, and his physical health by this stage was such that he tired easily. At a certain point he stopped trying to listen to the lecture. Instead he took out his rosary, and began — quite visibly — to pray it.

A few years before, Rahner had been having an argument with his friend, former student, and colleague Karl-Heinz Weger. They were talking about whether Rahner's philosophical arguments for the existence of God actually worked. "I always had something with which to counter, I always had an objection (and it was a serious matter for me)," Weger tells us. Once, however, the discussion became hopeless, Rahner brought the conversation to an end with the words: "I believe because I pray."[2] And indeed Rahner's first ever publication, at the age of twenty-two, had been a piece entitled "Why We Need to Pray" — a piece that stands as the prologue to this selection.

---

1. John Macquarrie, "The Anthropological Approach to Theology," *Heythrop Journal* 25 (1984): 272–87. This text includes a record of questions put by Rahner to Macquarrie on the basis of his lecture, and Macquarrie's replies.

2. "Ich glaube weil ich bete: Für Karl Rahner zum 80. Geburtstag," *Geist und Leben* 57 (1984): 48–52, at 51.

Karl Rahner (1904–84) was, of course, a formidably learned professional theologian as well as a Jesuit. He had held professorships at the Universities of Innsbruck, Munich, and Münster; he had been a significant influence on the Second Vatican Council; he was the recipient of many academic honors; his bibliography in German alone runs to more than fifteen hundred entries. But, as many of his admirers have come to realize, it was the experience of prayer that animated and inspired this scholarly activity. Rahner's theology was driven by a passion to articulate what the human person must be like if prayer is possible, if we human beings can really make contact with God. Rahner was indeed an important twentieth-century theologian, but only because he was more fundamentally a modern spiritual master.

Who Was Karl Rahner?

Born in 1904 to a pious family in Freiburg, a city in southwest Germany, Karl Rahner joined the Jesuits as an eighteen-year-old. After ten years of standard Jesuit training, he was ordained a priest in 1932. During his studies, he discovered a Belgian Jesuit philosopher named Joseph Maréchal (1878–1944), who had done some very difficult and controversial work on the interpretation of Thomas Aquinas, and was also keenly interested in mystical topics. Rahner also did an immense amount of private work on historical theology, especially on the history of penance and on the theology of prayer. This study was important. First, it gave Rahner a strong sense of how Christian theology had a history — a point that much public rhetoric in the Church denied, instead claiming to hand on in absolute purity the legacy given it by Jesus. Second, it gave Rahner and other Roman Catholic theologians of his generation a new and liberating way of understanding the concept of tradition. The people who call themselves traditionalists in any Church normally want to keep things the way they are. If, however, you understand that tradition has always been living, then the appeal to tradition can come to justify change.

As was normal at the time, Rahner continued in basic training for a further two years after ordination. Then in 1934 he went back to the town where he was born, Freiburg, to study for a doctorate in philosophy, where one of his professors was Martin Heidegger. After two years he produced a massive, enormously difficult book entitled *Spirit in the World,* a study of Thomas Aquinas's theory of knowledge. For reasons that are now obscure, it failed as a doctorate, even though it has now been published and translated into several languages. All was not lost however. On the side he was producing a second doctoral thesis, which he could submit to the faculty at Innsbruck (there was no residence requirement) in the same year, 1936. This second thesis is a study of patristic theologies of the Church and the Sacred Heart. It is a far slighter work, and the German original was published only recently.[3] It passed unproblematically.

Rahner then began to teach in Innsbruck and remained there until the Nazis closed the faculty in the autumn of 1939. During the war, he lived in Vienna, teaching on a freelance basis. He also lectured clandestinely for Jesuit students either in hiding from being called up into the Nazi forces, or else tucking theology lectures into their periods of leave. In the last year, he became a rural parish priest in Bavaria. After the war, he lectured briefly at the German Jesuit philosophy faculty in Munich and returned to Innsbruck in 1948, where he remained as a teacher of theology until 1964.

---

3. "E latere Christi": *Der Ursprung der Kirche als zweiter Eva aus der Seite Christi des zweiten Adam — Eine Untersuchung über den typologischen Sinn von Joh.19.34,* in *Karl Rahner Sämtliche Werke* 3:1–84. This collection will bring together Rahner's complete works in German in thirty-five volumes.

The major event of Rahner's later life was the Second Vatican Council, which took place between 1962 and 1965, having been called rather unexpectedly by Pope John XXIII in 1959. Rahner became a world figure only as a result of this council and the far-reaching changes in Roman Catholicism that it unleashed. By the time it opened he was sixty years old. He was fairly well known in the German-speaking world, but not outside it. He had never traveled outside Germany, Austria, and Holland until he was over fifty. But he was taken to Vatican II as an adviser by Franz König, then cardinal archbishop of Vienna. Once it became clear that the Council was to be creative, theologians such as Rahner and the French Yves Congar and Henri de Lubac became seminally important and influential — even though in the years immediately prior to the Council they had been suspect, indeed silenced. Rahner himself had had major difficulties getting a book published in 1962.

After the Council, Rahner threw himself into explaining the Council and promoting the conversion it called for. He became a symbol, a point of reference for a convulsive institutional change in an institution that had thought it could not change. His published output of shorter essays and lectures increased; he was given full secretarial support for the first time in his career, and he used it to the full. He became a kind of intellectual icon for the forces of change in Roman Catholicism, just as more recently Hans Urs von Balthasar has been taken over by those who claim that the Council was a mistake — an iconic use of both figures that in neither case is really justified by what they actually thought and wrote. Rahner became deeply admired, revered, even loved and idolized. In 1964, he moved from Innsbruck to a chair at Munich, and three years later to Münster, in northern Germany. He retired in 1971, at the standard age of sixty-seven, and then embarked on a hectic life of freelance writing and lecturing all over the world. In 1981, he retired back to Innsbruck and died there three years later.

Experience and Grace

Though lived Catholic spirituality even since the Renaissance and Reformation had often been rich and exuberant, the theology into which Karl Rahner was educated in the 1920s and 1930s was reticent about spiritual experience. It had been decisively shaped by a Counter-Reformation reaction against Protestantism, in particular against the possibility that a person's private experience of God could serve as a source of religious authority overriding the Church's official leaders. Thus standard Catholic theology tended to understand the presence of God among us as something in principle beyond our experience: we could only *believe* that it was true, on the basis of a message taught us by someone else. In an interview given a couple of months before he died in 1984, Rahner spoke of how he saw his theology differing from that of previous tradition in general and of his own teachers in particular:

> I have, in my own theology...over and over again drawn attention to how there is such a thing as the experience of grace. My teacher...Hermann Lange...was strongly opposed to this kind of thing. Lange did, relentlessly, defend the idea of a so-called "sanctifying, real [*seinshafte*] grace." However, in his view, this grace lay absolutely beyond consciousness. According to this tradition one could only know *about* it, through external revelation and sacred Scripture.[4]

Rahner argued for his alternative position in two ways. First, he appealed to Scripture and tradition: we are taught, quite simply, that God is God-with-us, that God establishes peace among us, that the fruits of the Spirit can and do make a difference to

---

4. *Glaube in winterlicher Zeit: Gespräche mit Karl Rahner aus den letzten Lebensjahren,* ed. Paul Imhof and Hubert Biallowons (Düsseldorf: Patmos, 1986), 29. The interview from which this quotation is taken was not included in the English version of this volume.

how we experience our lives. Second, the idea that grace (or anything else) could exist without *ever,* in *any* way, being in principle able to modify human awareness is self-contradictory; if you can speak of grace at all, you cannot be denying that you are aware of it, either in yourself or another, affecting your consciousness. If grace exists at all, it exists as a reality of human experience.[5] The experience may be very hard to name or recognize, and the reality of grace may not be accepted. But if God in Christ has become human, then, in the words of one of Rahner's early prayers, God has also become human experience. Rahner is insisting, therefore, not only that God dwells among human beings, but also that human awareness is capable of "touching our Creator and Lord."[6] For Rahner, this principle became central.

Theology and the Mystical

When Rahner was a young man, there was an acrimonious debate among Roman Catholic theologians about the nature of mysticism — by which was meant the actual experience of the realities of faith. Some started from the position put forward by Lange, but then modified it by construing the mystical as a special privilege — for these thinkers, mystics were by definition exceptions to the general rule that grace lay beyond experience. Others adopted a different line: any devout believer could in

---

5. For a much fuller and more technical development of these arguments, see Rahner's 1939 essay, "Some Implications of the Scholastic Concept of Uncreated Grace," *Theological Investigations* 1:321–46. In English, this collection runs to twenty-three volumes, published between 1961 and 1992 by Darton, Longman and Todd in London, and by Crossroad in New York.

6. Rahner adapts this phrase from Ignatius Loyola in the first piece he ever published, reproduced below as the Prologue to the anthology. The Ignatian echoes in this piece are thoroughly and convincingly discussed in Arno Zahlauer, *Karl Rahner und sein "produktives Vorbild" Ignatius von Loyola* (Innsbruck: Tyrolia, 1996), 86–93. For the general issue of Rahner's links with Ignatius, see also my *Karl Rahner and Ignatian Spirituality* (Oxford: Oxford University Press, 2001); Zahlauer's discussion is summarized on pp. 28–29.

principle attain to the mystical. What is important, however, for the understanding of Rahner's achievement is the assumption that both sides seem to have shared: that the mystical is the name simply of a *part*, normally an advanced part, of the life of faith and grace. For Rahner subverted the debate by at least implicitly challenging this assumption. If grace, the divine self-gift, is necessarily an experiential reality, then *all* grace is mystical. Moreover, if it is God's will that all human beings should be saved and come to a knowledge of God's truth (1 Tim. 2:4), God's grace must be present throughout the creation. Thus the language of mysticism offers an interpretation of the *whole* of human experience; it is not simply describing particular extraordinary experiences.[7]

For Rahner, therefore, "the mystical" and "spirituality" must be allowed to shape our understanding of theology, indeed of reality, *as a whole*. This was why he did not allow himself to become a conventional "spiritual writer" or "spiritual theologian." Instead he used what he learned from the great spiritual masters he studied as a young man — Ignatius Loyola, of course, but also writers from the early Church such as Evagrius and Gregory of Nyssa, and medieval spiritual writers such as Ruusbroec, Tauler, Eckhart, and Bonaventure — as inspiration for the study of theology as such. Spirituality was too important and too central to be a mere specialism.

As a theologian, Rahner sought to explain Christian beliefs by presenting them as consequences of his central conviction — an outrageous one once one stops to think about it — that human beings can experience God. Christian dogmas express different aspects of the reality we call God's self-disclosure in our experience, God's self-communication to human beings.

---

7. See the final piece in chapter 1, "The Mystical: The Way of Faith to God" (p. 61 below), where Rahner as an old man situates his own work in terms of this debate. Arguably, however, Rahner himself was not fully aware of how subversive his own position was.

They bring home to us what we are actually claiming when we say that our finite experience, shaped as it is by body, language, and society, shaped even by what Christianity calls sin, is also experience of our creator. If we can experience God, then God's own self must dwell within us, empowering this experience — otherwise we are simply creating an idol in our own image.

Moreover, this conviction of a *self*-giving God within our experience implies the doctrine of the Trinity. If we are relational beings, finding our identity in interaction with what is other than ourselves, outside ourselves, the "outrageous" doctrine of grace implies a doctrine of the one God as also three: the originating Father who remains transcendent, the Son who confronts us in the Word, and the Spirit who empowers our response.

Again, given the ambiguities of our own experience, Christian assurance demands that there must be a point in human history where the presence of God within us is somehow different, where our fragile life in God is seen as guaranteed. Christianity finds this assurance in the life, death, and resurrection of Jesus of Nazareth. Further, our means of communication with the guarantee that is Jesus Christ must themselves, derivatively, share his privileged status: hence doctrines of Church, of the inerrancy of Scripture, of the sacraments, of ordained ministry, and of the teaching authority within the Church.[8]

Vocation and Theology

Rahner seems to have been a private man. An extensive and helpful biography focusing on his external activities has been written,[9] and the archive of his books and papers in Innsbruck occupies two substantial offices. Relatively little, however, is

---

8. This style of argument is particularly illustrated by Rahner's 1959 essay "The Concept of Mystery in Catholic Theology," *Theological Investigations*, 4:36–73.

9. Karl H. Neufeld, *Die Brüder Rahner: Eine Biographie* (Freiburg: Herder, 1994); also available in Italian as *Hugo e Karl Rahner* (Rome: San Paolo, 1995).

available in terms of personal letters or diaries that would enable us to chart his emotional development, his sense of vocation, or his prayer life.[10] The notes that have survived from the Ignatian retreats he made during his training, for instance, simply record the talks that were given (in those days retreats were, of course, preached). Beyond the rather simple external facts — Jesuit formation, problematic doctorate, the war, various professorships, lionized retirement — his life history remains closed to us.

Perhaps, however, it is possible to highlight one important intellectual decision, made near the beginning of his teaching career. We have already looked at Rahner's central conviction about grace and mysticism — or, more abstractly, about how there can be no fundamental breach between what is real and what is experienced. The principle was also to guide him as he took his path through the multiple and arcane sensitivities that mark the internal politics of any theology faculty. When he arrived in Innsbruck, he found his own elder brother, Hugo, at the center of a movement for what was called "kerygmatic theology": — a second kind of theology existing alongside "academic" theology. Whereas "academic" theology would focus on the truth of God's own self, "kerygmatic" theology would work with different methods and focus more on the God who can be preached. It seems clear that Karl Rahner at least flirted with the movement; he published in its journal.[11] But, relatively early, he parted company with it. He came to deal with "kerygmatic" just as he dealt with "mystical": by claiming that a term often

---

10. But see the selection from the letters he wrote to Herbert Vorgrimler during the Council, reproduced in Vorgrimler's *Understanding Karl Rahner: An Introduction to His Life and Thought* (London: SCM Press, 1986 [1985]), 141–84. The novelist Luise Rinser published her letters to Rahner in *Gratwanderung: Briefe der Freundschaft an Karl Rahner 1962–1984* (Munich: Kösel, 1994) — but in the absence of Rahner's replies, no conclusions can be drawn from that work.

11. "Die deutsche protestantische Christologie der Gegenwart," *Theologie der Zeit* 1 (1936): 189–202. The text has been reproduced in *Karl Rahner Sämtliche Werke* 4:299–312.

used to designate *one part* of theology should properly refer to *an aspect of all* theology.

He reminisced on this decision twenty-five years later, in a brief dictionary article.[12] "Kerygmatic" theology was founded on assumptions that seemed ridiculous (at least to a believer) once you named them. The distinction between the two sorts of theology seemed to imply that God's own self was somehow different from the God-for-us proclaimed by the gospel. It also implied that you could know the truth about God without that truth somehow involving you, challenging you, transforming you:

> Rightly, this theory found no acceptance. *All* theology must be theology of salvation. It is impossible and illegitimate for there to be a theology that is merely "theoretical," fundamentally uncommitted.

While criticizing the movement — and by this stage (1961) it was a historical curiosity — Rahner nevertheless went on to highlight three important concerns that it represented:

> But this is not to gainsay a threefold basic concern underlying this initiative, a concern that is not yet satisfied:
>
> - a good part of contemporary scholastic theology does not stand sufficiently clearly in the service of a really living proclamation, meeting the human person of today and his or her faith-need.

---

12. *Lexikon für Theologie und Kirche,* 2nd ed., 6:126. Now reprinted in *Karl Rahner Sämtliche Werke* 17/1:313 (bullet points in the following quotation have been added). See also a fuller article that Rahner published in a Hungarian journal in 1941: "Über die Verkündigungstheologie," in *Karl Rahner Sämtliche Werke* 4:337–45. On the movement more generally, see Hugo Rahner, *A Theology of Proclamation,* trans. Richard Dimmler et al., adapted by Joseph Halpin (New York: Herder, 1967 [1939]).

- today's theological academic goings-on in the universities do too little to train the young pastoral clergy for their tasks.

- the kerygma itself cannot itself be a merely simplified version of academic theology, even if this theology is correct.

It is worth making two observations about this small article. First, though Rahner rejects "kerygmatic theology" (modern equivalents would be "pastoral theology" or "practical theology"), he identifies nevertheless three legitimate concerns informing the project. Rahner was not deaf to these concerns. An essay he wrote in the 1960s is entitled "The New Claims that Pastoral Theology Makes upon Theology as a Whole" — a title that says much about how Rahner understood his own intellectual vocation. He took the concerns behind "kerygmatic theology" as a stimulus to renew theology *as a whole*. That it is *human beings* who know the truth of God is not something theologically incidental, somehow independent of the content of that truth. God is God-with-us; God's reality incorporates us; and therefore our learning, our growth into the life of God, is constitutive of God's very identity. Moreover, when the word is preached effectively, when — for instance — someone truly hears the proclamation, "your sins are forgiven you," something new happens within the life history of that person. Theology may indeed be able to name this reality, but it cannot determine in advance what it will be and how it will play itself out. For each person's history is unique and unrepeatable: the word of God is still alive and active.

Second, Rahner's grounds for denying the legitimacy of a "kerygmatic" theology are not the standard ones. Plenty of theological academics, even now, are sniffy about the "pastoral" aspects of theology. "Pastoralia" — to use a quaint word still current in the UK — is often patronized as a soft under-belly of theology, somewhat suspect in comparison to the hard, objective study of Bible and dogma. But Rahner's objection is different: he is challenging the claim of *any* theology to "objectivity," or, better, insisting that theology is always more than objective. If theology is about the incomprehensible God who is yet *our* God on whom we depend, it cannot simply operate with the methods and conventions of an Enlightenment science like Newtonian physics, which presupposes a "neutral" observer and operates with objective facts. Rahner was not challenging the distinction between theology-in-itself and theology-for-people because he was worried about theology-for-people being somehow too subjective, too difficult to handle. He wanted, rather, to insist that — at least in a Christian account of the matter — theology-for-people is the only theology there is: the study of a God who is permanently and irrevocably God-with-us. It is the assumptions behind "academic" or "scholarly" theology that need to be questioned. Once those illusions are exposed, the only problem with "practical theology" or "kerygmatic theology" is that the adjectives add no real content to the noun.

The issues about "kerygmatic theology" and "pastoral theology" apply also to what in English is a newer term, although now much in vogue: "spirituality." It is not that Rahner was *both* a modern theological master *and* a modern spiritual master as a kind of extra, by coincidence as it were. Rather, the reflective activity we call theology, and the emotional and relational process we call spiritual growth, are two aspects of one fundamental reality: the growth of the whole human person toward God. Because theology is a self-implicating discipline, a creative theology will have "spiritual" meaning: people who read it and hear it aright will be challenged by it, changed by it. Good spiritual direction helps people make a decent theology out of their own experience — however much defensive resistance to the Spirit often takes the form of "intellectualization." Conversely, even if a mainstream "spiritual" figure, an Ignatius or a Thérèse, writes in a crude, theologically uneducated way, the very fact that they are prophetic and creative implies that they set an agenda for *theology.* What makes them different from the holy people to be found both within and outside any Christian community is that their experience and writings enable us somehow to break new ground in *understanding* and *knowing* God.

The Church in which Rahner grew up often fulminated about the errors of the modern world. But it was nevertheless influenced — unconsciously — by the enormous success of science in the Enlightenment period and tended to take the kind of objectivity proper to nineteenth-century science as the standard for all possible truth. Even when it claimed to receive a divine revelation, the kind of truth revelation delivered was often presented as if it were simply a set of facts, different only because the Spirit of God somehow substituted for scientific discovery. But there are fundamental differences in kind between statements like "Jesus is the Son of God" and "Jesus lived in Palestine." You can locate Palestine, and you can determine whether or not Jesus lived there, whatever you think about Jesus: it is straightforwardly an objective fact that our minds can comprehend. But "Jesus is the Son of God," is a different kind of sentence. It is metaphorical. "Metaphorical" does not mean "untrue" or "merely subjective." When we say that athletes are at the peak of their fitness, or that Amelia is head-over-heels in love with Percival, we are making factual claims. But they depend on metaphors, which communicate because those who hear or read such claims "get it." Somehow we have to recognize the metaphor for what it is, to become open to the shared understanding out of which the expression comes. The principle applies to religious claims. "Jesus is the Son of God" is a factual claim; its truth does not depend on whether or not people believe

it. But we understand how "son" works here only by recognizing its place within a tradition of commitment, faith, and
practice, involving surrender to one whom we can never fully
"comprehend."

By recognizing that our response to grace is a moment in
the life of grace itself, by recognizing that we know God's own
reality as an inexhaustible mystery that encompasses our whole
being, Rahner was thus committed to developing theology as
a discipline with its own integrity, methods, and approaches to
truth. If we consider him in terms of the classifications common in theology today, he fits into no category. He is regularly
studied in courses on dogma, on fundamental theology, on philosophy of religion, on moral theology, on spirituality, and on
pastoral theology. But he does not fit easily under any of these
headings, and in all these fields his contributions in one way
or another are subversive. For example, one of his most important works, the early *Hearer of the Word,* is presented as a
study in *Wissenschaftstheorie.* There is no English translation of
this word — the conventional "philosophy of science" is wide
of the mark: it means something like the theory of how the
different academic disciplines relate. Rahner is rethinking the
relationship between God and knowledge in general, in ways
that theologians — let alone ordinary language — have still to
catch up with fully. Liberation theologians sometimes present
Rahner as an example of illusion-ridden abstract thinking, and
advocates of a theology in touch with postmodernism sometimes claim that Rahner's theology is still too much wedded
to metaphysical categories and untenable grand narratives.[13]

---

13. For example: "Rahner's most characteristic theological profundities are
embedded in an extremely mentalist-individualist epistemology of unmistakably
Cartesian provenance. Central to his whole theology...is the possibility for the
individual to occupy a standpoint beyond...immersion in the bodily, the historical
and the institutional" (Fergus Kerr, *Theology after Wittgenstein* [Oxford: Blackwell,
1986], 14). Contrast a 1972 statement of Rahner's: "My Christianity is...anything
but an 'explanation' of the world and of my existence; it is rather the prohibition

But, once you filter out the irrationalist excesses of both movements,[14] Rahner is probably both a liberation and a postmodern
theologian *avant la lettre.*

Experience, Faith, and Secularity

The point can also be made less abstractly. Rahner's central
insight about grace and experience was developed within the
narrow world of neoscholastic seminary theology. Nevertheless,
that insight led Rahner to move beyond the ghetto and to answer quite new questions about faith that were arising in a
society beginning to secularize. Particularly through his experiences of Vienna during the devastation of World War II, Rahner
became aware of how conventional social structures were col-
lapsing and of how faith needed a new kind of support. It is
in these terms that Rahner explains what he is doing when he
writes his late masterpiece, *Foundations of Christian Faith:*

> The person who comes to theology today...does not gen-
> erally feel entirely at home in a faith that can be taken

against regarding any experience, any understanding...as finally and definitively
valid, as completely intelligible in themselves" ("Why Am I a Christian Today," in
The Practice of Faith: A Handbook of Contemporary Spirituality, ed. Karl Lehmann
and Albert Raffelt [London: SCM, 1985]). Kerr has subsequently acknowledged the
force of the counterdefense in R. R. Reno, *The Ordinary Transformed: Karl Rahner
and the Christian Vision of Transcendence* (Grand Rapids, Mich.: Wm. Eerdmans,
1995). See too Thomas M. Kelly, *Theology at the Void: The Retrieval of Experience* (Notre Dame, Ind.: University of Notre Dame Press, 2002), for a good attempt
to distinguish Rahner's achievement from what is standardly attacked by critics of
"liberal" theology.

14. There are clear connections between the movements in European theology
of which Rahner was a part, and the beginnings of liberation theology. Ignacio Ellacuría learned much from Rahner. But the wholesale abandonment of metaphysical
thinking left Rahner, surely rightly, protesting about what he called "Jesuanity" (*Jesuanismus*) — a devotion to the figure of Jesus that simply left aside any claims
about his identity with God. Christianity has some connection with the mystery that
creates and sustains the world. "I was actually in Frankfurt when [Ernesto] Carde-
nal explained that the kingdom of God had broken into Nicaragua, that there were
no more prisons there and they all loved one another....I want nothing to do with
such rubbish" (*Faith in a Wintry Season: Conversations and Interviews with Karl
Rahner in the Last Years of His Life* [New York: Crossroad, 1990 (1978)], 51).

24 KARL RAHNER

for granted, supported by a homogeneous religious milieu common to everyone. Even a theology student among the young has a faith that is contested and challenged, a faith that is far from taken for granted, a faith always to be struggled for anew, a faith that still has to be built up. And they need not be ashamed of this.[15]

Moreover, Rahner also became increasingly aware of how all fields of academic study, including the different branches of theology, had advanced to such a complexity that no one could possibly be competent in every field relevant to the understanding of the Christian faith: philosophy, biblical studies, the human sciences, history, archaeology, languages, and so on. Two of the passages in chapter 4 of this anthology, from Rahner's old age, explore this theme in rather mellow, informal language: the passages on the unnamed virtue and on intellectual patience. But the theme can be found early in Rahner's writing, certainly in the 1950s,[16] and was the driving concern behind *Foundations of Christian Faith*. Faith therefore had to be grounded in some other way, through an "unscientific" or "unscholarly" approach.[17]

"Tomorrow's devout person will either be a mystic — someone who has 'experienced' something — or else they will no longer be devout at all."[18] We misunderstand this famous sentence if we take it as a claim that future Christians must be like John of the Cross. For Rahner, we need to lose the sense of elitism associated with talk of the mystical. His point, rather, is that "spirituality" must now, in our cultural setting, be central to any attempt to make Christianity plausible or live it out

15. *Foundations of Christian Faith,* trans. William V. Dych (London: Darton, Longman and Todd, 1978 [1976]), 5.

16. "The Student of Theology: The Problem of His [sic] Training Today" (1954), in *Mission and Grace,* 3 vols. (London: Sheed and Ward, 1963–66), 2:147–81.

17. *Foundations of Christian Faith,* 3–14.

18. "Christian Living Today and Formerly" (1966), in *Theological Investigations,* 7:3–24, at 15.

with integrity. Rahner came to appeal to the unbeliever, not by claiming that it was somehow irrational or a logical mistake not to accept the whole Christian package (the strategy, unsuccessfully pursued, of seminary fundamental theology), but rather by simply presenting the Christian message, trusting that God's grace is given to all human beings, and hence that the message might converge with a person's lived experience. We can offer the Christian interpretation of human existence, presupposing that the reality of which we are speaking is already present, latently, in those to whom we speak:

> And each person is then asked whether they can recognize themselves in the person trying through the message of Christianity to express their self-understanding, or else whether they can responsibly set as their own truth, before themselves and their own lived reality, the conviction that they are not the sort of person that Christianity promises them they are.[19]

Experience and Church

Such an appeal to people's experience of God implies a rich, diversified vision of Church authority — another theme that the fourth chapter of this anthology explores. Church authority does not reside simply in the officeholders. The life of grace reaches ever fuller expressions as the members of the Church interact, each out of the grace latent and realized, accepted and rejected, within them. Moreover, given that it is the will of God that all human beings be saved, the beginnings of grace and of religious insight must be present in all human beings, whether or not they call themselves Christian. The security, the assurance offered by the Church is that of a promise that God has

---

19. *Foundations of Christian Faith*, 25, see 231–32; for further background, see Endean, *Karl Rahner and Ignatian Spirituality*, 222–37.

definitively begun to bring about the Kingdom, and that God will definitively establish it. Rahner remains a radically Catholic theologian: grace transforms a human reality that is relational, and the life of grace is thus essentially corporate. But this richer, more diversified account of authority undermines the besetting temptation of modern Roman Catholics to equate ecclesial fidelity with passive toadyism. It is abundantly possible — and in no way excluded by the divine promise — for officeholders to err, for the Church to sin, for dissent from authority's directives to be not only permissible but obligatory. Not surprisingly, therefore, a certain sort of hierarchical imagination has always been uneasy with Rahner's theology.

Someone who has learned from Rahner may still be horrified by scandals of the kind that that are currently emerging regarding sexual abuse in the Church. But there is absolutely no reason for their faith to be shaken. If we have an investment in more triumphalist accounts of the Church, we will be tempted to deny reality: the idea that the Church can be corrupt will threaten our worldview. Rahner's account of the Church's inviolate holiness centers on divine promise as to what will be, not on present human achievement. As such it provides a resource for a fully Catholic insistence on Church and tradition that remains realistic about human reality.

Concentration and Dialogue

In one way, therefore, Rahner's theology — for all its verbal difficulty and intellectual subtlety — is profoundly simple. He is seeking to integrate the whole of Christian theology around one simple message: that God is a God of self-gift, a self-gift that can, however dimly and incompletely, be experienced. To refer all Christian doctrine, therefore, to the experience of God has the effect of concentrating and simplifying theology. At the same time, however, it opens that theology to a permanent process of growth, interchange, and transformation. For if God's self-disclosure is continuing in human experience, then it will not be finished until God is all in all. The dogmas of tradition exist not as truths complete in themselves, but rather as resources for helping us discover the ever greater glory — another Ignatian echo — of the God whose gift of self pervades all possible experience. Human knowledge of God — even under grace, even indeed Jesus' awareness of his own divine identity and of his Father — is permanently a "preliminary knowledge," a *Vorgriff:* we can never comprehend or grasp God, but only continue to explore the transcendent as disclosed in our continuing experience.

This is how Rahner expressed the principle at the beginning of his first major essay on Christology:

> Ultimately, an individual human recognition of truth only makes sense as a beginning, a promise, of the recognition of God — and this latter, whether in the beatific vision or elsewhere, can only be genuine and a source of blessing when it is recognized as something ungraspable, at the point where the act of apprehension and the act of limitation specifying the thing known surpass themselves and move into what is ungrasped and unlimited. All the more so does any truth about the *self*-revealing God open us up into what cannot be beheld: it is the beginning of what is limitless. The clearest and most lucid formulation, the holiest formula, the classical concentration of the Church's centuries of work in prayer, thought, and struggle about the mysteries of God — these draw their life, then, from the fact that they are beginning and not end, means and not goal, *one* truth that makes freedom for *the* — ever greater — Truth.[20]

---

20. "Current Problems in Christology" (1954), in *Theological Investigations,* 1:149–200, at 149.

It follows, therefore, that the proclamation of the gospel is permanently interactive: no one is untouched by the grace of God, and the proclaimed message will be heard aright only if it somehow interacts — in ways that might be surprising, creative, or unprecedented — with the self-gift of God already present. It follows, too, that Christianity is permanently growing and in process: Christian fidelity is not a matter simply of preserving a heritage unsullied, but rather of courageous engagement with what is new, with what seems strange.

Thus a theology originating in abstruse scholastic discussions about grace and mysticism provided Roman Catholicism in the middle decades of the twentieth century with an important resource, enabling it to overcome its deep-rooted defensiveness about "the modern world" and to engage in creative dialogue. Intellectual and cultural developments of the last centuries — biblical criticism, evolutionary theory, the awareness of non-Christian religions, the growth of historical consciousness — have had an unsettling effect on Christian belief, calling into question what previous generations felt able to take as read. In reaction all branches of Christianity seem tempted to indulge in a tedious and misguided conflict between traditionalism and liberalism. Rahner's approach to grace, spirituality, and experience helps us avoid this trap. If our access to God lies through our experience — and through all our experience, not just our peak moments — then our access to God, though assured, is an access to one whom we must continue discovering. What Christianity is committed to, then, is not the claim that its traditions possess the whole truth, incontrovertibly, but rather the claim that its traditions possess one resource among others — admittedly a privileged and indispensable one — for *continuing to discover* God's truth. Perhaps only when it is understood in these terms can Christianity be an intellectually responsible option.

Rahner's work is often said now to be superseded. Some regard its generous account of God's presence in the world

as naively romantic and its implicit relativizing of current
Christian practice as a form of apostasy; others find Rahner
insufficiently attentive to the searching questions raised by postmodern thought, in particular by the latter's insistence that all
religious expression is socially constructed; still others find that
his inclusiveness is still too centered on Christianity to be of
real use in a world of religious pluralism. Even, however, if
these criticisms were to be justified — a point that there is no
need to concede — Rahner still teaches us something of vital
importance about how we find the God of Jesus Christ, the
Word made flesh, precisely *in,* not despite, our everyday human
experience. Such a vision demands patience and maturity, and
perhaps Roman Catholic experience since Vatican II suggests
that institutions and churches cannot easily maintain such virtues. But — to adapt Chesterton's *bon mot* on the Christian
ideal — the problem is not that Rahner's theology and spiritual
vision have been tried and found wanting: they have been found
difficult and left untried.[21]

A wise and venerable Irish theologian is reported to have said
this: "In all the many books Rahner has written, he is really saying only one thing — but it is maddeningly difficult to say what
that one thing is." Perhaps we can take this observation one
step further. If all Rahner's writing arises from a conviction that
God is present in experience, this renders his work profoundly
unitary, profoundly single. But at the same time, this vision also
yields a very *untidy* account of God. The God who speaks in
our experience, the God who is in our experience, must be as
unsystematic and chaotic and pluriform as we are. In the end
any theology worthy of the name must be a mixture of a clarity reducing everything to first principles and an openness to a
God of freedom, who will be who God will be for us into our

---

21. G. K. Chesterton, *What's Wrong with the World* (London: Cassell, 1910), 39.

unknown future. These are qualities for which Rahner's work remains outstanding.

•

The extracts from Rahner's works that follow are divided into four main chapters. The first illustrates Rahner's passionate belief about God's presence in human experience *as a whole*. The second presents texts about how we can grow in our appropriation of that presence, in particular through the decisions we make and through a properly Christian attitude to suffering. The radical inclusiveness of Rahner's vision leads him to understand the role of Jesus in a distinctive way, which the third chapter explains and demonstrates. The final chapter points up the permanent unfinishedness inherent in Rahner's theological vision, with particular reference to the problem of evil and suffering, and to life in the Church.

Rahner's language is often technical; his thought patterns are difficult; his texts were often prepared rather poorly for the press. For these reasons, the texts that follow come supported with rather more editorial material than is normal in this Modern Spiritual Masters series, and considerable work has been done to clarify the translations. Nevertheless, some of the details will inevitably remain obscure. When that happens, it is probably best just to pass over and read on; the difficult expression is unlikely to be central. For Rahner's message is in the end a simple and accessible one: an appeal to recognize and appropriate God's self-gift, the mystery that Christianity calls grace. And this reality is at least latent in every human mind and heart.

Prologue

Why We Need to Pray

This reflection was published when Rahner was twenty-two years old, the first piece of his to appear in print. It is hardly a literary masterpiece, but it is nevertheless striking how insistently the youthful Rahner stresses the human person's potential for contact with God's own self. There are also echoes of the Ignatian Exercises: the sense that there are practical lessons to be learned from the moment "when God's Spirit filled you," and the reference to the Creator and Lord embracing "his" devout soul into his service and praise (Exercises n. 15).

What should your heart be like?

It should be like what the Holy One, the Eternal One willed, when, through His gift, you came to be, like how He is drawing you, teaching you, admonishing you in His holy grace.

It should be like Christ's heart, full of love, and of sacred, sacrificing power.

It should be like what you yourself yearned for when God's Spirit filled you, when your vision about your life and your life's task became clearer, and you longed for love, which can accomplish all things and which understands all things, when you longed for the strength to be everything for others, for the strength to abandon yourself and to serve others....

31

Look, that's what you should be like. Think again what it
   means that the God past all grasp wills for you to be holy,
   what it means that the one who died did this as an example
   for you, what it means that your own heart's desire is to
   become holy ... and then ask:
Is your heart like that?
Is God's will reality and truth in you?
Is your inner self renewed in Christ Jesus?
Is your heart driving forward into life? ...
How can you do this? Really do it? Faithful always, without
   half-measures or faint-heartedness?
You must pray. We must pray!
If we don't pray, we remain attached to earthly things, we become small like them, narrow like them, we get pressured by
   them, we sell ourselves to them — because we give our love
   and our heart to them.
We must pray!
Then we are far away from the petty everyday that makes us
   small and narrow. Then we draw near to God and become
   capable "of touching our Creator and Lord."
"Draw near to God, and He will draw near to you" (James
   4:8). Yet where He is communicating Himself to his creature
   and embracing it into His love and His praise, He is having
   the soul recognize how null, how empty, and how weak it
   is, filled with the nullities of its narrow existence, full of fear
   at the pain and suffering of the cross, full of petty pride and
   narrow self-seeking....
But then, in His own time, when it pleases Him, He makes the
   soul bright, enlightened, so that it can understand God's will,
   God's ways, so that it longs for a heart of faith, full of sturdy
   hope, full of love that never ends, so that it longs for a heart
   that is open and selfless and pure.
Then the Lord fills "His" soul with the power of grace, so that
   its deeds fulfill the desires and promises of its prayer, so that

it becomes strong enough to accomplish all things and endure all things.

Then HE gives it the Spirit of God, "which comes to help us in our weakness,"

the Spirit that loves it, so that it can forget desires shaped by the world's love,

the Spirit that consoles it with His joy,

the Spirit that is the soul's "first fruits of eternal life."

Look, that's what a heart is like when it prays. For the person who draws near to God — they become one Spirit with HIM. But God's Spirit is "LOVE, JOY, PATIENCE, KINDNESS, FAITHFULNESS, GENTLENESS, SELF-CONTROL" (Gal. 5:22–23).

That's what our heart becomes if we pray in the Spirit of God.

— *Sehnsucht nach dem geheimnisvollen Gott,* 78–80

1

God and Human Experience

"I encountered God; I experienced God's own self." This was the insistent, passionate refrain of an extraordinary piece of writing published by Rahner in 1978. Rahner was here adopting the persona of Ignatius Loyola (1491–1556), founder of the Society of Jesus, speaking from heaven to one of his modern followers. Nevertheless, he was really expressing his own central convictions. In an interview shortly before his death he confirmed that this piece could be seen as his "spiritual testament — if one may use such sentimental terms."[1]

Rahner here reads the life of Ignatius in terms of his own theology. For Rahner, Ignatius discovered a dimension of the gospel message that had never previously been articulated clearly, and the book entitled Spiritual Exercises *represented Ignatius's attempt at enabling others to make the same discovery for themselves. Rahner presents Ignatius's conversion experiences, on his sickbed at Loyola and then in the solitude of Manresa, as the unfolding of a potential latent in all human beings: the capacity to find God's own self in experience. This reality of God is communicated in what theology calls grace and invites us to a*

---

1. *Bekenntnisse: Rückblick auf 80 Jahre,* ed. Georg Sporschill (Vienna: Herold, 1984), 58.

total trustful surrender of our own being — a surrender most obviously apparent in how we regard our own inevitable death.

The frustration Ignatius experienced at the hands of the Inquisition in Spain led him to study liberal arts and theology in Paris, an experience that for Rahner underlines the ecclesiastical tensions implicit in how Ignatius understood human experience of God. Such experience at once fosters a closer relationship with the Church, and yet also relativizes its authority; for us, nearly half a millennium later, the Ignatian experience of God can help us see the present decline in the Church's external prestige and influence not as disaster but as purification.

ENCOUNTER WITH GOD

The Immediate Experience of God

As you know, I wanted — as I used to say then — to "help souls": in other words, to say something to people about God and God's grace, and about Jesus Christ, the crucified and risen one, that would open up and redeem their freedom into God's. I wanted to say this just as it had always been said in the Church, and yet I thought — and this opinion was true — that I could say what was old in a new way. Why? I was convinced that I had encountered God, at first incipiently during my sickness at Loyola and then decisively during my time as a hermit at Manresa; and I wanted to communicate such experience to others as best one could.

When I make this sort of claim to have experienced God immediately, this assertion does not need to be linked to a theological disquisition on the essence of this kind of immediate experience of God. Nor do I want to talk about all the phenomena that accompany such experiences — phenomena that of course have their own histories and their own distinctive characteristics. I'm not talking about pictorial visions, symbols, words heard; I'm not talking about the gift of tears and the like. I'm just saying that I experienced God, the nameless and unsearchable one, silent yet near, in the Trinity that is His turning to me. I have also experienced God — and indeed principally — beyond all pictorial imagining. God, who, when He comes to us out of His own self in grace, just cannot be mistaken for anything else.

Such a conviction perhaps sounds innocuous in your pious trade, working as it does with the most elevated words available. But fundamentally it is outrageous: outrageous for me from where I am, in the past-all-graspness[2] of God that is experienced here in a quite different way again; outrageous for the godlessness of your own time, a godlessness that is actually in the end only doing away with the idols — idols that the previous age, with an innocence that was at the same time appalling, equated with the ineffable God. Why shouldn't I say that this godlessness extends right into the Church? After all, the Church throughout its history, in union with the crucified one, is meant to be what happens when the gods are abolished.

Were you never actually shocked by what I said in my *Reminiscences:* that my mysticism had given me such certainty in my faith that it would remain unshaken even were there no Holy Scripture?[3] Wouldn't it be easy enough here to make accusations of subjectivist mysticism, and of disloyalty to the Church? For me, actually, it wasn't so surprising that people in Alcalá, Salamanca, and elsewhere suspected me of being an illuminist,

---

2. *Unbegreiflich* and its cognates are generally translated in this selection with expressions centered on "past all grasp." Rahner is drawing on the vocabulary here of the German mystics; it seems appropriate for an English translator to use a phrase of Hopkins: "past all/Grasp God" — ("The Wreck of the *Deutschland*," stanza 32).

3. Ignatius, *Reminiscences* (Autobiography), n. 28: "if there weren't Scripture to teach us these matters of the faith, he would be resolved to die for them solely on the basis of what he has seen."

or *alumbrado*. I really encountered God, the true and living one, the one who merits this name that destroys all names. Whether you call this kind of experience mysticism or something else doesn't matter here. Your theologians might like to speculate how it can be somehow explained in human concepts that something like this is possible at all. Why such immediacy doesn't take away a relationship to Jesus and hence to the Church is something I'll talk about later.

But first: I encountered God; I experienced God's self. Even then, I could already distinguish between God's self and the words, the images, the particular limited experiences that somehow point to God. This experience of mine obviously had its own history. It began in a small and modest way. I spoke and wrote about it in a way that now I too, obviously, find endearingly childish, and that conveys what is really meant only very indirectly and from a distance. But the truth remains: from Manresa onward I experienced in increasing measure and ever more purely the modeless[4] past-all-graspness of God.

[...][5]

Godself. Godself I experienced — not human words about God. God, and the sovereign freedom that is proper to God, the freedom that can only be experienced as coming from God, not from the intersection of earthly realities and calculations. [...] That's what it was, I say. Indeed, I would say this: you can have the same experience too, if you allow your skepticism — driven as it is by an underlying atheism — about such a claim to reach its limit, not just in eloquently expressed theory but also in actual bitter experience. For then something happens. Death, for all that we carry on living biologically, is experienced as *either* a radical hope *or* as absolute despair. And in this moment, God

---

4. Another technical term from German mysticism: God is beyond all categories of being.

5. Ellipses enclosed in brackets represent the editor's omissions; those without brackets represent ellipses in the original.

offers God's own self. (No wonder I stood just at the edge of
suicide at Manresa.)[6]

A Pedagogy toward a Distinctive, Personal Experience

This experience may be grace, but that does not mean that
anyone is in principle excluded from it. Of that I was just convinced. I certainly didn't think that the grace of Manresa in my
subsequent life up to the loneliness of my death, when I was
quite on my own,[7] was a special privilege for a chosen, elite individual. That was why I gave Exercises whenever this kind of
offer of spiritual help looked as if it might be accepted. I even
gave Exercises before I'd studied your theology and had managed with some effort (I laugh) a master's degree from Paris.
And also before I had received priestly and sacramental power
from the Church. And why not? The director of the Exercises
(as you called him or her later) is not, if you bear in mind what
these Exercises are ultimately about, passing on the word of the
Church as such in an official fashion — for all that these Exercises are linked to the Church. They are just giving (when
they can) support from a distance, very circumspectly, so that
God and humanity can really meet immediately. The first companions I had can only be described as very varied in their
gift for this; and before Paris all those I wanted to win for
my plans through the Exercises ran away even from me. I put
the question again. Is it *so* obvious that something like this exists, legitimately exists? Was it obvious for the churched culture

---

6. Ignatius, *Reminiscences,* n. 24: "there often used to come over him, with
great impetus, temptations to throw himself out of a large opening that the room
he was in had."

7. Hugo Rahner had written a striking meditation on the fact that Ignatius died
alone, without the sacraments of the dying: "The Death of Ignatius: 1556" (1956),
in *Ignatius: The Man and the Priest,* trans. John V. Coyne (Rome: CIS, 1982), 107–
23.

of my time? Is it obvious for the atheism of yours? Obvious enough for it not to have been rejected in the old days as an anti-Church subjectivism and in your modernity as illusion and ideology?

In Paris I added the Rules for Thinking with the Church to the Exercises. I contested successfully all the canonical processes that people kept burdening me with. I subjected my work and that of my companions directly to the wishes of the pope. About this I must speak more fully later. But the truth remains: God is able and willing to deal immediately with His creature; the fact that this occurs is something that human beings can experience happening; they can apprehend the sovereign disposing of God's freedom over their lives and appropriate it — a disposing that objective argument "from below" cannot predict as a law of human reason, neither philosophically, theologically, nor arguing from experience.

Ignatian Spirituality

This quite simple-minded, and yet in fact quite outrageous conviction seems to me (together with what I'm going to talk about) the heart of what you tend to call my spirituality. If we look at it in terms of the history of church devotion, is it old or new? Obvious or shocking? Does it mark the beginning of "modernity" in the Church? Does it perhaps have more in common with the foundational experiences of Luther and Descartes than you Jesuits for centuries have wanted to admit? Is it something that is going to recede again from the Church of today and tomorrow, a Church in which, almost, people can no longer bear silent solitude before God and instead seek to flee into an ecclesiastical collectivity — even though in fact a Church community can only be built up from spiritually aware people who have really met God, not from those who use the Church in order ultimately to have nothing to do with God and God's free past-all-graspness? My friend, for me questions like this have now ceased, and therefore need no answer. Where I am now, I am no prophet of the Church's future history. But you must ask yourselves these questions, and answer them, at once in clear theology and in decisions about your own history.

The fact, however, remains: humanity can experience God's own self. And your pastoral care must have this goal in sight always, at every step, remorselessly. If you just fill up the storehouses of people's consciousnesses with your theology, however learned and up-to-date it is, in a way that ultimately engenders nothing but a fearful torrent of words; if you just train people for devotion to the Church, as enthusiastic subjects of the ecclesiastical establishment; if you just make the people in the Church obedient subjects of a distant God represented by an ecclesiastical hierarchy; if you don't help people get beyond all this; if you don't help them finally to abandon all tangible assurances and isolated insights and go with confidence into that past-all-graspness where there are no more paths, accomplishing this in a love and joy beyond measure, first in life's situations of ultimate, inescapable terror, and then — radically and ultimately — also in death, in company with the Jesus who died in Godforsakenness — if you don't do this, then, in what you call your pastoral care and missionary vocation, you'll have either forgotten or betrayed my "spirituality."

All human beings are sinners and short-sighted. Not infrequently, therefore, you Jesuits have, in my opinion, sinned through such forgetfulness and betrayal. Not infrequently, you have defended the Church as if it were the ultimate, as if ultimately it were not, where it is true to its own essence, an event — an event of human beings giving themselves to God, and in the end no longer needing to know what they are doing. For God is indeed the mystery past all grasp, and only as such can be our goal and our blessedness.

I should now say more expressly — particularly for you repressed, covert atheists of today — how a person can meet God
immediately like this, up to the full development of this experience, where God then meets a person in everything, and not
just in special "mystical" moments, and when everything, without getting submerged, becomes transparent toward God. I also
really need to talk about situations that are particularly helpful for fostering such experiences (i.e., when such experiences
are had clearly for the first time). In your time, these do not
necessarily have to look like what I tried to set up through
the hints in my Exercises, even thought I'm also convinced that
these Exercises in your time too, taken pretty literally, can still
be more successful than some fashionable "improved versions"
that people here and there put forward. I also need to make
it clearer that the awakening of such divine experience is not
in fact indoctrination with something previously not present in
the human person, but rather a more explicit self-appropriation,
the free acceptance of a reality of the human constitution that
is always there, normally buried and repressed, but nevertheless
there inevitably. Its name is grace, and God's own self is there,
immediately.

Perhaps I need to tell you (this is a funny business) that you
have no need to run off like people desperately thirsty to East-
ern sources of meditation, as if the sources of living water were
no longer to be found among us — though neither may you say
in your arrogance that it is only human wisdom about the depth
of things that can come from these sources, not the real grace
of God. But I can't talk further about all that now. What is actually at stake in the experience that I'm talking about is the
heart — the heart that surrenders itself in faith and hope, and
that loves its neighbor.

— "Ignatius of Loyola Speaks to a Modern Jesuit," 11–15

Rahner's late spiritual writing draws on ideas he developed at the very beginning of his career. Encounters with Silence *is a collection of prayers initially published in a magazine for Austrian priests in 1937; they appeared as a book as a means of meeting the losses anticipated by the publishers of Rahner's failed philosophical dissertation,* Spirit in the World. *In one of the prayers, "God of Knowledge," Rahner writes movingly of God's direct presence within himself even as a small baby. "Your Word" — the word that is Christ — "has become my experience."*

GOD'S WORD AND A BABY'S EXPERIENCE

Thanks be to your mercy, you infinite God, that I don't just know *about* you with concepts and words, but have experienced *you*, lived *you*, suffered *you*. Because the first and last experience of my life is you. Yes, really you yourself, not the concept of you, not your name that we give you. For you have come over me in the water and the Spirit of baptism. Then there was nothing that I thought out or excogitated about you. Then my reason with its flip cleverness was still silent. Then you became, without asking me, the fate of my heart. You took hold of me — it wasn't that I "comprehended" you;[8] you transformed my being right down to its ultimate roots and origins, you made me a sharer in your being and life, you gave yourself to me — you yourself, not just a distant, fuzzy report about you in human words.

So I can never forget you because you have become the most intimate center of my being. If you are living in me, it is not just pale and empty words about anything and everything that haunt my spirit, which, in their profusion and confusion only

---

8. Du hast mich ergriffen — nicht ich dich "begriffen."

fuddle my heart and make my mind tired. In baptism, you, Father, have spoken your Word into my being through and through, the Word that was before all things, more real than they, the Word in which alone all reality and all life first comes to be.... This Word, in which alone there is life, has become through your action, God of grace, my experience. [...]

Admittedly this Word that, having been born consubstantially from your heart, has been spoken into my heart — admittedly this Word still needs to be interpreted for me by the external word that is appropriated in faith through hearing. As yet your living Word is dark for me; as yet it is only softly, like a distant echo from the utmost depths of my heart into which you have spoken it, that it reverberates into the forefront of my conscious living — the forefront where my knowledge parades itself, the knowledge that brings about discontent and mental exhaustion, the knowledge that becomes nothing more than the bitter experience of being forgotten and deserving to be forgotten, because in itself it will never become union and life. And yet, behind this fatigue and mental exhaustion another "knowledge" in me is already, now, grace-filled reality: your Word and your eternal light.

— "God of Knowledge," in *Encounters with Silence*, 30–32

When Rahner's Ignatius says that he encountered God, he is not, ultimately, reporting some privileged particular experience of encounter, but rather an "experiential discovery that humanity is always in a state of having already encountered God, and continues to encounter God." Rahner is locating the holy in human experience as a whole. Two points are important here. First, Rahner is insisting that God's self in grace is present throughout creation. Jesus, the Church, and Christian tradition obviously have a particular importance, but they are not the only places where God's grace can be found. This conviction has far-reaching theological and practical implications, and we will explore these in later chapters of this book. Second, Rahner is challenging a widespread tendency for Christians to regard the holy as somehow distant from us. Because this tendency is so rampant, Rahner needs to challenge it by finding a new way of speaking, but the message is as old as the Hebrew Scriptures:

> *Surely, this commandment that I am commanding you today is not too hard for you, nor is it too far away. It is not in heaven, that you should say, "Who will go up to heaven for us, and get it for us so that we may hear it and observe it?" Neither is it beyond the sea, that you should say, "Who will cross to the other side of the sea for us, and get it for us so that we may hear it and observe it?" No, the word is very near to you; it is in your mouth and in your heart for you to observe. (Deut. 30:11–14)*

The remaining passages in this chapter illustrate how Rahner's vision leads him to challenge some rooted Christian habits. The next, from another prayer in Encounters with Silence, *speaks of how God is to be found not in special practices, but in daily routine: our life feels distant from God, not because God is distant, but because our hearts need to be awakened and converted.*

GOD OF MY DAILY DRUDGE[9]

I should like to bring my daily drudge before you, O Lord — the long hours and days crammed with everything else but you. Look at this daily drudge, my gentle God, you who are merciful to us men and women for whom daily drudge is virtually all we are. Look at my soul, which is virtually nothing but a street on

---

9. This word is the general translation adopted for *Alltag* — which is more negative than "everyday."

which the world's baggage-cart rolls along with its innumerable trivialities, with its gossip and fuss, with its nosiness and empty pretension. In face of you and your incorruptible truth, isn't my soul like a market, where junk dealers from every direction come together and sell the wretched riches of this world, a market where I, and indeed the world and his wife, are spreading sheer nothings in permanent, benumbing restlessness? [...]

But how am I meant to convert this daily drudge of my neediness, how am I to convert myself to the one thing needful that you are? How am I supposed to get away from daily drudge? Isn't it you who has pushed me into this daily drudge. When I first began to realize that my true life, ordered to you, mustn't suffocate in the daily drudge, wasn't I already lost amid the world and within my daily drudge? Isn't it as a human being that you have made me? [...]

And look, my God, if I did want to run away from my daily drudge, if I did want to become a Carthusian so as to have nothing else to do but remain in silent adoration before your holy face, would I then really be raised beyond the daily drudge? When I think of the hours that I spend at your altar or saying your Church's office, then I realize that it's not worldly business that make my days a drudge, but me — I can change even these sacred actions into hours of drudgery. It's *me* who makes my days drudgery, not the other way round. And thus I realize that if there can ever be a way for me to you, then it leads through my daily drudge. To get away to you without my daily drudge is something I could do only if, in this holy escape, I could leave myself behind.

But is there a route through the drudge to you? Doesn't this kind of route lead me ever further away from you, ever deeper into the noisy void of busyness, where you, silent God, do not have your dwelling? I am well aware that eventually we get fed up with the business that fills our lives and our hearts. I am well aware of the tiredness of life that philosophers talk about, and

of the sense of satiety that your word tells us was your patriarchs' final experience. I am well aware that this will be more
and more my lot, and indeed that drudgery becomes in the end
of its own accord a massive depression about life in general. But
surely pagans experience this as well? Can we really say we have
arrived in your presence when the daily drudge finally shows its
true colors, when it proclaims that all is vanity and a chasing
after wind, when I have the same experience as your preacher
in Ecclesiastes? Is it in this simple sense that daily drudge is the
way to you? Or isn't this rather the drudge's final victory, when
a burnt out heart ends up seeing the things of its own daily
drudge as all the same, things that can so easily otherwise help
people to overcome the heart's boredom and monotony? Is it
really the case that a tired and disappointed heart is closer to
you than a fresh and joyful one?

So then, where are you to be found, if the enjoyment of
the everyday makes us forget you, and if the disappointments
of the everyday have not yet found you? Indeed when they've
made the heart so bitter and sick that it's even less able to find
you? My God, if we can lose you in everything — if neither
prayer, nor a sacred celebration, nor the silence of the cloister,
nor disillusionment about everything in general can of themselves forestall this danger, then even these holy, non-everyday
things still belong to the daily drudge. Indeed, it's not that the
daily round is a part of my life, or even the largest part of my
life. It's always daily drudge, everything is daily drudge, because
everything can ruin for me the one reality that is necessary, and
deprive me of it: the reality that is you, my God.

But — if there is nowhere where you have given me a place to
which we can just flee away in order to find you, and if everything can be the loss of you, the One, then I must also be able to
find you in everything. Otherwise, humanity couldn't find you
at all — humanity that cannot exist without you. Therefore I

must seek you in everything. Each day is daily drudge, *and* each day is your day, the hour of your grace.

So, my God, I come to understand again what in fact I've known for ages. What my mind has so often told me is now coming to life again in my heart. But what's the point of the mind's truth if it isn't also the life of the heart? I must keep on taking out the little note I made many years ago, copied out of Ruusbroec, and reading it again, since the heart is also continually taking it on board. I'm always consoled to read how this spiritual man imagined his life; and the fact that I still love these words after so much daily drudge in my life is like a promise that you will eventually bless my daily drudge too.

God comes without cease in us, with intermediary and without intermediary, and demands of us enjoyment and activity — and demanding that they should not constrain, but confirm each other. Thus inward persons possess their life in these two modes: rest and activity. And they are present wholly and undividedly in both. For they are completely in God — they are resting in enjoyment — and they are completely in themselves — they are serving in loving activity. And at all times they are charged and urged by God to be renewing both, rest and activity. This is what it is for a human person to be just, to be on the way to God with inward love and constant activity. Persons move into God through their enjoying desire in eternal rest. And they remain in God, yet nevertheless move out to all creatures in all-embracing love, in virtues and in justice. And this is the highest stage of the interior life. All those who don't have rest and activity as one reality have not yet reached this justice. This just person cannot be constrained through their recollection, since they turn inward both in enjoyment and in activity. Rather, they are like a two-sided mirror, picking up images on both sides. For with

the highest part of their spirit, people receive God together
with all His gifts; and with the lower parts, they pick up
bodily images through the senses.... [10]

I must live out the daily drudge and the day that is yours as
one reality. As I turn outward to the world, I must turn inward
toward you, and possess you, the only One, in everything. But
how does my daily drudge become the day that is yours? My
God, only through you. Only through you can I be an "inward"
person. Only through you am I with you within myself even as I
am turning outward in order to be among things. Neither *Angst*
nor nothingness nor death free me from being lost in the things
of the world — to use ideas from modern philosophy — but only
your love, love for you, you who are the goal drawing all things,
you who satisfy, you who are sufficient to yourself. Your love,
my infinite God, the love for you that passes through their heart
and extends out beyond them into your infinite expanses, your
love that can still take in everything that is lost as the song of
praise to your infinity. For you, all multiplicity is one; all that
is dispersed is gathered into you; everything outside becomes
in your love something still interior. In your love, all turning
outward to the daily drudge becomes a retreat into your unity,
which is eternal life.

But this love that lets the daily drudge be the daily drudge
and yet transforms it into a day of recollection with you — this
love only you can give me. What then am I to say to you now,
as I am bringing myself, the bedrudged, into your presence?
I can only stammer a request for your most commonplace of
gifts, which is also your greatest: the gift of your love. Touch
my heart with your grace. Let me, as I grasp after the things of

---

10. Ruusbroec, *Spiritual Espousals*, b 1932–1960. Rahner has cut the text. The
translation here comes from Rahner's German rather than the middle Dutch original. A translation from the original can be found in Jan van Ruusbroec, *The
Spiritual Espousals*, trans. Helen Rolfson (Collegeville, Minn.: Liturgical Press,
1995), 107.

this world in joy or in pain grasp and love *you* through them, the primordial ground of them all. You who are love, give me love, give me yourself, so that all my days may eventually flow into the one day of your eternal life.

— "God of My Daily Routine,"
in *Encounters with Silence*, 45–52

Another way in which we are tempted to confine the holy is by identifying it with the soul, and hence despising the body. The passage that follows was written by Rahner in the form of a sermon by the medieval German mystic Johannes Tauler: Rahner used to tease his Innsbruck students by reading it out during a lecture on grace, and then challenging them to guess the author. Rahner here insists on what we would now call a holistic spirituality of the body. As in the prayer about the daily drudge, Rahner insists that the problem of sin is not to be resolved by escape from our humanness or by marginalizing some aspect of our daily existence. Rather, we have to rely on God's healing power, a power that works through the whole of our complex reality, through our bodies as well as through our souls and spirits.

A SPIRITUAL DISCOURSE
ON DESIRE AND CONCUPISCENCE
in the Style of Master Johannes Tauler

St. Paul begins and speaks thus: "The flesh desires against the spirit and the spirit against the flesh." This is a dark word, and many people have not grasped it rightly — and so it has become a problem for them. They've thought: "One must hate the body, because it's said here that the flesh kicks against the spirit." Mark what I say, and I speak it with confidence, even if one without understanding believes I am contradicting St. Paul. This is what I say to you:

You must love the body. Why am I saying "body"? You must love yourselves. But that always includes the body. When, therefore, I say you must love the body, I am not thereby saying, "You must love yourself and then in addition yet another thing, something which is as such not part of you." What I'm saying, rather, is a command for only the one thing: love yourselves just as God, in His pure wisdom and fathomless love, has willed to create you, namely, as human beings. See, my children, you are always fully involved in everything that occurs in you, both outwardly and inwardly. As you rejoice in God our Savior, so your heart and your flesh rejoice, as the prophet says. Do not believe the secret heretics, who in their wickedness or ignorance speak to you like this: "If you want to find your God, then you must go far away from your body." Wickedness and ignorance! Hasn't the Word become flesh, then? Isn't that the reason why she who carried him in her motherly womb is blessed among women? Wasn't this why she received him in her pure heart?

Now, of course, our flesh can certainly, on its pilgrim way to our God, become dry, as the psalmist says. But when that happens, it doesn't mean that our spirit is enraptured. No — both are yearning, the body and the spirit, as in a purgatory for the waters of grace. Again I say — and this is the other side of the coin — as long as you are burning with sinful passion, don't say, "This is my body, and my spirit has nothing to do with it." That's what the covert heretics of our day say. No, you yourselves with body and spirit have given occasion to evil desires, and God will visit you, body and soul together, with His judgment.

But then, against my word, you say this within your heart: "I've not provided any occasion for it, and yet it has come into me. I haven't lit nor fanned the fire, and yet sinful lust burns

in me." You're right. But understand rightly what you are saying. When this kind of contradiction happens in you, it's not
that the body is at war with the spirit, but rather that your
whole humanity is divided against itself, and at odds. Hear
what St. Augustine says: "It is not the flesh, that you [he is
praying to God] have created, but the corruption, the pressures
and temptations of the flesh that are a prison for me" (*Enna-
rationes in Psalmos*, 141:17). So speaks the holy doctor. And
I say in addition: "Don't the pressures and temptations affect
body and spirit alike? Yes, the spirit as well?" So then, the body
is divided from the body and at war with itself, but also the
soul from the soul. The whole man is divided in two, ever since
we all sinned in Adam. See, for him everything was still one
and undivided. When he was good, he was good with all his
powers of body and spirit in pure unity. When he was evil, he
was evil in just the same way, in other words completely. His
whole essence and all his powers spoke in him: *non serviam* —
I won't be a servant of God. And therefore his sin was greater
than all sins, and nothing else like it has ever been heard of in
this sinful world.

But the faculty with which God endowed Adam in Paradise
is called by the masters the gift of integrity. This is a power
and a faculty that make a person skilful and nimble in doing
the good and in desiring God — doing this in a manner so
powerful and integrated that they do what they do, they love
and serve God, without division, doubt, or doubleness. Nothing in them remains dark; nothing remains that is not inflamed
by the bright fire of their love; no desire still resists, sluggishly
and maliciously, the design of such integrated love.

Ah, beloved brother: just as Adam was once endowed inwardly, so are we once again to become. We are not yet like
this. For in us the flesh still desires against the spirit, as St. Paul
says (and now you grasp what he means by this). But there already burns in the innermost citadel of our spirit the light that

the Holy Spirit has inflamed. And in as much as good and honest persons, amid all pressure and temptation, remain true all their life long, so they will become ever more undivided and integrated in body and soul in the love and service of God, just as it was for Adam. Their spirit and flesh will bear in peace the sweet yoke of the Lord and rejoice in the Savior.

Hear this too, I dare to say: were persons to become so integrated and undivided in themselves as Adam was, and therefore have their love and service fixed not on themselves but on God, such persons could not but die the blessed death that Mary did (which is no death at all). And they could beget many children of grace, as Adam could have done. So then, let us become again one and integrated in the inner person. The more integrated we are in ourselves, the more we are at one with God, who is nothing but pure unity, far beyond all division or dispersion. May our Lord, who is mighty and good, grant us to be capable of this. Amen.

—*Sehnsucht nach dem geheimnisvollen Gott, 82–85*

To be human is to change, to be moving. Given what philosophy tells us of God's unchangeableness, we can easily imagine that to become holy is to become a radically different sort of being, a changeless being. In the next passage, from a whimsical yet profound collection first published in 1964 and called Everyday Things, *Rahner challenges this idea. To be human is to be on the move; and we encounter God only because God moves toward us in the* Word. *Indeed God is the secret principle behind even our constant movement: not only the goal but also the way.*

ON MOVEMENT

Movement is one of the most everyday things in our daily round. We only think about it when we can't move any more, when we're shut in or paralyzed. Then we suddenly experience being able to move as a grace and a miracle. We're not plants, tied down to just one setting determined for us; we search out our setting for ourselves, we change it, we make a choice — to move. And as we change, we experience ourselves as beings who change ourselves, as searchers, as those who are still on the way. We recognize that we want to move toward a goal, and that we don't want to wander into a mere vacuum. When we are moving toward something difficult and unavoidable, we still experience ourselves as free, even if we can only move toward accepting it as something imposed.

We talk about a way of life, and the first description of Christians was as "those who belonged to the way" (Acts 9:2). When Scripture tells us that we are not to be hearers of the word but also doers of the word, it is thereby also saying that we don't just live in the Spirit, but should move in the Spirit. We talk about the *course* of events, from the good out*come* of an undertaking, about the *approach* to understanding, of how a deceitful person *goes behind one's back,* of something happening as an *occurrence* (from the Latin for "runs across"), of a change as a *transition,* of the end as *a passing away.* A king *ascends* to a throne; our life is a *pilgrimage;* history *moves forward;* something we understand we call *accessible;* a decision can appear as a *step.* Both in the sacred and the secular spheres, great celebrations are marked by processions and parades.

These few, quite tiny indications are enough to show how we are constantly interpreting our whole life in terms of the utterly basic experience of everyday movement. We move, and this simple physiological movement is already enough to say that we have here no abiding city, that we are on the way, that our real arrival is still ahead of us, that we are still seeking the goal, that we are really pilgrims, wanderers between two worlds, humanity in transition, moved and being moved, steering a movement already imposed on us, and also discovering, as we plan our moves, that we don't always end up where we planned to.

In the simplest act of movement — for acts presuppose knowledge and freedom — what it is to be human is in fact fully present, and we are faced with our own existence. A Christian's faith reveals what the goal of this existence is and promises that it is coming. We exist as an unending movement, conscious of itself and of its unfinishedness, a movement that searches, and that believes it finds, because (and again we cannot speak otherwise) God's own self *comes* in the descent and return of the Lord, who is our future to come.

We move; we cannot but be seeking. But the Real and the Ultimate is coming to us, and seeking us out — obviously only as we are moving, as we are coming-toward. And when the time comes that we have found — found because we have been found — we will discover that our very coming-toward was already being carried (this is what we call grace) by the power of the movement that is coming upon us, by God's movement toward us. — *Everyday Things*, 9–11

As the previous passage shows through its discussion of "movement," a term with roots in Aristotle and Thomas Aquinas, Rahner's spirituality is often cast in an idiom influenced by his philosophy. We can, obviously, explain the changing reality of our being human in any number of ways: through history, psychology, genetics, sociology, ethnography, and so on. Whenever we do this, however, we have a consciousness of something more: a consciousness that we are doing this, a consciousness of self that somehow transcends all these explanations (Rahner calls this level of self-awareness simply "transcendence"). Thus we are in the world, and the product of indefinitely many causal forces; equally, we are not confined to the world in the way a material object is. Our awareness transcends the networks of causality that make us what we are, and involves a permanent questioning about what makes things be — a question whose answer we can never grasp, but can nevertheless call "God." Rahner's spiritual vision depends primarily on Christian revelation — a revelation that Rahner interprets as saying that God is not simply a distant "term of transcendence," but rather one who, without ceasing to be wholly Other, wholly beyond our comprehension, has come near to us, and through Christ and the Spirit invested himself in us.

The next passage comes from a set of retreat conferences that Rahner gave to students at Innsbruck immediately before their ordination to the priesthood. It reflects on the "Contemplation to Attain Love," which Ignatius puts at the end of his Spiritual Exercises, in particular on why it is that we can "find God in all things" and "in all things love and serve the Divine Majesty." Christianity's talk of human beings in intimacy with God makes sense only as a consequence of the Incarnation: the assertion that one who is of our flesh is also divine. It follows that we must be careful how we understand the idea of the mind and heart ascending to God. For God's own self in Christ is permanently present to the lost of this world, and we find union with God, therefore, primarily through sharing in his self-emptying descent. It is worth noting that one of the students who first heard this retreat conference was Ignacio Ellacuría, the distinguished philosopher who was to be martyred in El Salvador in 1989.

LOVE

Theologically it is all well and good that we talk of creatures returning to God. Quite true though this is, there is still something more to be said. The reason we can really find God is that God has not just created the world — rather, God's own self — for all that God is the God of inaccessible light — has, in

His eternal Word, eternally descended into the world. In other words, we find God because God, by Himself with His own reality "descending," has lost himself as love into His creation, never again to leave it.

Always remember that it is probably — to put it carefully — only in and through the Incarnation of the Word that the immediacy of the beatific vision is possible. For, if that were not the case, how could the sheer immediacy of the vision, its lack of anything to mediate it, not be the sort of immediacy that would just burn up the whole creature as it came to know. Don't we necessarily vanish to the extent that we draw near to God? If that's not so, why can we settle ourselves, so to speak, in the absolute, infinite, incomprehensible, searing light of God's own self — we who are creatures? How come that this creature, which is radically finite, is yet *capax infiniti,* itself receptive to the infinite as such? Of course we know that God is past all grasp, infinite mystery — but to *live* and *experience* God in His past-all-graspness, as this immediacy: how can anything like this occur at all?

In the last analysis, a minimal condition for this to be possible is that God as such, without ceasing to be God, can make a gift of self to the world. This means, again as a minimal condition, that the Incarnation of the eternal Word amounts to God becoming worldly, God stepping out of Godself as love — the fundamental truth of God's own self, of what God's own self actually does, of what God's own self can do. But this means that immediate love for God, love so immediate that God in God's own life and glory becomes the content of our creaturely lives — that love is possible only because God has descended into the world. From that it follows that our "ascending" love to God is always a participation in God's descent to the world.

If love, therefore, is possible only with and within the self-emptying of divine love into the world, and if this is the real structure of our love for God, than all this is possible only

through the kingdom of Christ, in discipleship of Christ, who
is precisely the Word who descends into the world. It can only
be a participation in his fate, and hence, specifically, also only a
participation in his passion; it can only be his love, his love that
must go right through the Third Week.[11] But if such love is a
participation in the movement of divine love into the world in
Christ, then for this reason it must be a love of God within the
world and within the Church. For this reason it becomes — as
we are told in the meditations on love — service.

This does not mean simply that we have to prove our love
in a crude sense — as if God was able to read off the truth and
reality of our attitude only from what we did exteriorly and
was unable also to look into our hearts. It is rather that our
love is, as Ignatius says,[12] essentially our appropriation of this
divine love (for, of course, this love of ours for God is the yes to
his love for us). But this love of God is precisely the descending
love, the love that communicates itself to the world, the love
that, as it were, loses itself in the world, the love that brings
about the becoming-flesh of the Word, the love that means the
abiding of the eternal Word in his creature, and that therefore
also means a divinized world and Church.

But whoever is participating in the action of the divine love
for us, this action of descent into the world — participating because their own love is appropriating this divine love — must
therefore be serving: they must be seeking to make their love
real in this objective way, in the world. Then this service is not
some external proof of something that, in itself, is independent
of this proof; rather, this love is service-with-God-in-descent,
descent into the otherness, the lostness, the sinfulness of this
world. For this reason, the *amor* of which Ignatius speaks is
really in the characteristically New Testament sense *agape*, not

---

11. The part of the *Spiritual Exercises* devoted to Christ's passion.

12. In the "Contemplation to Attain Love," our prayer of love ("Take, Lord,
receive . . .") is presented as a response to the active, creative love of God.

eros.[13] It is not an expression of craving poverty, reaching from below to above, but rather a love that has, along with the divine glory and life and strength, already been given. It is only this love that gives the proper theological grounding for this "finding God in all things."

Why can we find God in all things? Because God — precisely as the eternal glory and vitality that can never be confused with the world — this God as such has made a gift of self to the world. This "seeking and finding God in all things" is not a philosophical truth, nor a spiritualization of the mind's simply experiencing its transcendence through the necessary mediation of finite objects. Were that so, our task would simply be to transcend, simply to be indifferent. Then we would need, as it were, permanently to be keeping our distance, maintaining a standoffish attitude to the world, so as to be, as it were, philosophers wanting to find God. Or else we would have to say that we know only indirectly something about God, that we can sense the creator only as we sense His finite gifts and take them to ourselves. God would only ever be the one who was silently worshiped as a distant horizon and from a distance, without anyone actually being able to speak religiously about Him.

But the Christian, who participates in God's action of descent to the world and of love for this world — a love in which God has accepted the world definitively, for all eternity, as his ownmost reality, as the expression of himself — can, in this love, love with a radicality that would not otherwise be possible or imaginable for a human being. Christians can do this despite all indifference, despite all reserve, despite all crucifying death in Christ. No one can turn themselves so radically in love toward the world as the one who does it in this descent of God's —

---

13. Rahner is here picking up on different Greek words meaning "love," discussed by such authors as Anders Nygren (*Agape and Eros*) and C. S. Lewis (*The Four Loves*). *Eros* is seen as somehow less disinterested, more driven by our own needs, that the Pauline term, *agape*.

God who has, in Jesus Christ, accepted for always and for eternity the flesh of humanity and thus of the world (all, obviously, in its proper place and order).

Therefore this love, as Ignatius describes it, moves out into the world through work and service, just as the Exercises demand of us. The question keeps coming up; we are constantly being called to labor with Christ. This love, therefore, is always looking away from itself. It does not lose self-awareness, but neither is it an awareness marked by sublime spiritual introversion; rather people find their own selves by serving, laboring, going outward — losing oneself in the service of others. Since this love seeks not self but God, and God's world into which God has loved Himself and lost Himself, it can always be transformed by God. Since this love does not seek self, and since therefore this love does not make itself the measure of all things (for it forgets itself in the giving), it can always let God be greater than everything else, greater indeed than itself. Thus it can be and remain reverence, praise and service,[14] a love used as an instrument of service in the redemption of the world. Thus this love knows that closeness to God increases the more the sense of difference grows, and that the paradoxical mystery of our relationship to God is this: that humility and love, distance and closeness, being totally at God's disposal and acting oneself — these grow not in inverse but in direct proportion.

— from "Love," in *Meditations on Priestly Life*, 270–74

The final extract in this chapter is taken from what seems to be a transcript of a tape-recording made in 1978. Spontaneously, without self-censorship, Rahner is differentiating his own understanding of God's presence in all human experience from other accounts of faith and mysticism. If the mystical is

---

14. An allusion to Ignatius, *Exercises*, no. 23.

a reality of all human experience, then a theology of the mystical is in the end unconcerned with spectacular phenomena and skeptical about divine "intervention." It is also radically anti-elitist; the mystical is located not in unusual deeds, but simply in the reality of the self, created by God and sustained by God's self-giving grace. Once again, Rahner makes reference to Ignatius's Spiritual Exercises — the recording is roughly contemporary with "Ignatius of Loyola Speaks to a Modern Jesuit."

THE MYSTICAL:
THE WAY OF FAITH TO GOD

Are visionary experiences really what we mean by the mystical and by experience of God, or are they rather phenomena (however much they are to be taken seriously) accompanying a more fundamental kind of experience of God? If we go for the latter, how are we to understand this experience of God? Actually — in my opinion — it's quite obvious that with Ignatius's mystical experiences, which lasted even into his later years, this pictorial, visionary stuff was not for him what it was really about, nor could it have been. Persons with a visual imagination can bring themselves — or can be brought by others — to see Jesus in the flesh, painting in the details one way or another. This happens in the Exercises in the so-called Application of the Senses, and to a certain extent you can train yourself in the skill. Whether this is still possible for us today, and what we should make of all this — that's another question. But, conversely, this also goes to show that the real religious and existential heart of visionary experiences like this is in no way to be sought in these pictorial, visual phenomena. The old, classical mystical theology was well aware of this. When a shining, rosy-cheeked Jesus

appeared to Teresa of Avila, adorned with pearls, this theology used to say that it wasn't actually Jesus coming down from
heaven and appearing as he actually is in himself. What's going on here, rather, is that God is bringing about an imaginary
reality. Here theology was faced with a simple question: What's
happening when Baby Jesus appears to St. Anthony of Padua,
given that objectively Baby Jesus has simply ceased to exist? In
the end this can only be an imaginary vision; in the end too, the
imaginary and pictorial can also be brought about by purely
natural means.

With the genuinely mystical, the decisive, central thing is not
the imaginative reality: rather something more radical, something deeper is going on in the core of the person — deeper than
the things we can more easily describe but that in the end are
only imaginative and are thus freighted with all the marks of
the visionary's personality. To put it crudely, Jesus hasn't got a
heart surrounded by the crown of thorns. When St. Margaret
Mary Alacoque nevertheless sees this, and Jesus appears to her
showing his heart, then we've clearly got an imaginative vision.
The mystics also note that the real and central mystical reality
is the miracle that lies *behind* this kind of imaginative thing. If
this central reality isn't there, then the imaginative of itself is
simply natural and of no religious interest.

*Rahner goes on to discuss the great Carmelites Teresa of Avila
and John of the Cross, and then Ignatius. He alludes to the
so-called "Principle and Foundation" of the Spiritual Exercises
(no. 23): the statement that humanity is created "for the praise,
reverence, and service of God," and hence that all else is of
secondary importance. Thus we need to be "indifferent to all
created things . . . so that, on our part, we want not health rather
than sickness, riches rather than poverty, honor rather than dis-
honor, long rather than short life . . . desiring and choosing only*

what is most conducive for us to the end for which we are created."

Rahner links this teaching to the claim that Ignatius speaks of a "consolation without object." As an interpretation of Ignatius, this statement is controversial and questionable. Be that as it may, Rahner uses this claim, in combination with his philosophical concept of "transcendence," to make important points about how the mystical is an element simply in the experience of everyday faith, indeed of being human.

...Perhaps we need to see indifference far, far less (this hasn't, I don't think, been done yet at all) as simply a moral task, and still less as a reasoned moral decision, articulated in words, to be indifferent here and now to all things on the face of the earth. Such a decision indicates, naturally, a good intention to be indifferent, but it isn't indifference. It's when individuals, so to speak, set aside the particular realities that make up their existence — at every level of their being and their personality — that indifference begins. In the Principle and Foundation, Ignatius has his eye on this just as a goal. But the full reality is attained only through the whole process of the Weeks of the Exercises.... It's the same when I find another person repulsive, with every fiber of my being, and then decide: no, I want to behave kindly toward this person, I want to like this person. This is perhaps a useful resolution; perhaps I'm setting a worthwhile goal. But it's still a long way from the point where my whole being has changed into spontaneous sympathy for this wretch whom, humanly speaking, I've hated up till then.

It's like this with indifference. Putting a distance, existentially withdrawing from the individual reality of my being — this isn't something about which I can just say the word and it's done. It's rather a difficult, slow mystical development. When this at least slowly begins, when there's death, renunciation, when the taken-for-grantedness of the world crumbles in a night of the senses and of the spirit, it's then that a person slowly — now we can use philosophical language again — senses and experiences what human transcendence oriented to God really is, experiences it as something more than the inevitable condition that makes possible our everyday dealings with the world.

[...] This is the real, mystical, fundamental experience of God. And this account of the matter, of course, evades the basic difficulty: namely, that we can't suppose anymore — or at least can't convincingly show — that God intervenes at a particular point in space and time in the stream of consciousness. Mystical experience is not the product of a divine intervention in space and time. Rather it's the becoming ever more radically self-aware — a process obviously directed by God's providence — of human transcendence as absolute openness to reality as such, to the personal God, to the absolute mystery.

One mustn't think that this understanding of the mystical — as a point where the experience of transcendence becomes self-aware — makes the really mystical experience of God something natural. Quite the contrary: obviously this experience of transcendence is always in fact sustained by God's *self*-imparting. Through what we call the Holy Spirit, grace, the supernatural virtues of faith, hope, and love, this transcendence is radicalized: it becomes something that can really approach God. Through grace, human transcendence ceases to be just what makes everyday intercourse with the world possible; it also ceases to be directed just to an ever-receding goal that we never attain called God. Rather, this transcendence receives a promise from God, in God's gracious, Spirit-laden self-communication, that it will reach this goal. And wherever individuals, — what I'm saying now is basically outrageous — can dare, as wretched creatures, to speak with God in person, tap God on the shoulder as it were and expect that there will be a response, then they're asserting their transcendence as a transcendence radicalized by God's anticipating grace, a grace permanently present at least in the form of an offer to our freedom, and in which God is experienced "from within," beyond images. Obviously this experience of God isn't yet the beatific vision; at that point there's a qualitatively different immediacy in the encounter with God. Nevertheless, the New Testament itself speaks of grace as the "first fruits of the spirit," a kind of down payment of the infinitely close and just unsurpassable encounter with God in the "beatific vision."

What can a person of the future, a young person today, do in order to arrive at this basic experience, this insight? To start with, there will have to be change in the Church's attitude to the question of how extraordinary the mystical is. Of course there are visions and levitations and insights — even in the mysticism of those who first expressed the Church's tradition itself — that are evidently not part of the normal mental furniture of the average Christian. Seventy or eighty years ago, there were fierce arguments in the Catholic theology of mysticism as to whether the real essence of the mystical was a special grace, accessible only to particular individuals — one that could be absent even when individuals dedicated themselves, in the language of the time, to the way of perfection and made a lot of progress along it by the exercise of "heroic" virtue. In other words, people argued whether the mystical was an extraordinary way of salvation, intended only for a few, or was invariably, and more or less consciously, an essential element of Christian life and Christian perfection. Our Jesuit, Fr. Poulain, declared that the mystical was something quite extraordinary, not experienced by ordinary mortals. Against him were Dominicans and various theologians who thought differently on this question. I think that a sensible person has to be against Poulain, on biblical grounds and because of the theology of grace and of faith. It's not that the mystics are one step higher than those who believe; rather, the mystical at its actual theological heart is an intrinsic, essential aspect of faith (not the other way round).

If you think about these things, then you have to say that initiation into Christianity is ultimately initiation into the mystical — to use biblical language, from Galatians for example, initiation into the experience of God's Spirit. The mystical is not a special event. When Paul says "you foolish Galatians" (Gal. 3:1), he's taking it for granted that the experience of the Spirit should make it clear to them that they are justified by Jesus Christ and not by the works of the Law. This reference to the experience of the Spirit must also be something that can still exist today.

What answers, however, do we get from exegetes, preachers, teachers about the question of how we experience the Spirit? Even today, we surely need some reasonable account of where and how this experience of the Spirit can be had among us — even if only with difficulty and after a lot of mental rubbish has been cleared out. About a year ago I heard a lecture by a Protestant exegete. He was using biblical language quite naively, talking about the Spirit and the experience of the Spirit in Luke. And he never asked himself the question in this lecture where something like this was to be found among us. I can't today carry on, just because I'm a follower of Christ, interpreting every vaguely benevolent feeling as an experience of the Spirit.

Nevertheless, a theology of the experience of the Spirit is absolutely necessary, whether or not one develops it as a theology of the mystical. I've got to be able to say to people today: it can happen and it does happen, in you — perhaps repressed, unnoticed, perhaps not really accepted by you in existential freedom. But you can have it, and with it you have an experience of God — an experience in which God is present in your consciousness not just because a verbal word about God is there, indoctrinated from outside. Rather something else is there, something more fundamental.

— from "Mystik — Weg des Glaubens zu Gott,"
in *Horizonte der Religiosität,* 19–24

2

Turning Points

Rahner may believe that God is permanently present to us, but this certainly does not mean he sees our spiritual life as serene, untroubled enjoyment of a changeless grace. God may be closer to us than we are to ourselves, but it is still the task of a lifetime for us to appropriate that presence, to understand and accept that the whole of our being is enfolded within the persons of the self-communicating God.

Writing in the early 1980s to a young man who was a chronic depressive, Rahner offered some tentative advice:

> *You say, "I believe in God." Try taking this sentence seriously, making it a reality. Even if you do this, perhaps this God will nevertheless, perhaps, be expecting you to live a difficult, tough life. But why not? We can't seek out a life for ourselves just as we like, following whatever our problematic wishes. We must accept ourselves, just as we are. But when we really do this — do it honestly, courageously, and in hope — then we are accepting God's own self.*[1]

"God has no other sign, no other light in our darkened world, than Christ to be our brother."[2] *That line of the Dutch*

---

1. *Is Christian Life Possible Today?* 65.
2. Reference taken from the musical setting, "Trust What You See," by Bill Tamblyn (Colchester: Chiswick Music, 1976). Tamblyn refers to Huub Oosterhuis,

*liturgical poet Huub Oosterhuis reminds us that the Christian
life is never a matter of making God any more present to us
than God is already. Our task, rather, is gradually to recognize this presence, gradually to entrust ourselves to it. God is
always within, and ultimately the Church can only unfold that
reality. We can begin this chapter with a passage in which the
elderly Rahner imagines Ignatius talking about the Church and
about ministry. No gospel, no sacrament is of any use unless it
interacts with a presence of God already there within the self.*

RELIGIOUS INSTITUTION
AND EXPERIENCE FROM WITHIN

I'd just like to clarify what I've been referring to a bit more with
an image. Think of the heart as the soil. Is this soil to be condemned forever to barrenness? Is it a desert where the demons
have their home? Or is it fertile land that brings forth eternity's
fruits? The Church — so it can seem to us — sets up enormous
and complicated irrigation systems in order to make the heart's
soil fertile, through its Word, its sacraments, its institutions, and
its practices. Now, all these "irrigation systems" — if one can
put it this way — are certainly good and necessary (even granted
that the Church itself admits that the heart's soil can also bring
forth the fruits of eternity in situations where the Church's "irrigation systems" haven't made headway). Of course the image
is misleading; obviously there are elements in what the Church
does through gospel and sacraments with a logic and rationale that this image doesn't clarify. But still, let's stay with this
image. Then what I'm saying appears like this: besides these waters coming from outside, piped from outside that are meant

---

"A Christmas Carol," in *Your Word Is Near,* trans. N. D. Smith (Paramus, N.J.:
Paulist, 1968).

to irrigate the soul's soil (or — abandoning the image — besides religious indoctrination, over and above statements about God and His commandments, over and above everything that merely points *to* God as a reality other than itself — and here belong Church, Scripture, sacraments etc.), there is a source, so to speak, drilled deep within the land itself. And so from this kind of source, drilled within, from the heart of the land itself, the waters of the living Spirit well up into eternal life — just in fact as it says in John.

As I said, the image is misleading. In the end you can't play off this spring within against the "irrigation system" from outside; and obviously these two realities affect each other. Every call (another image) from outside in God's name exists only to make clear God's self-expression and self-promise within; and this latter also needs that call in some earthly form — though this form can also be far more varied and restrained than your theologians of an earlier time allowed, and though such a call from outside, a call of responsibility, of love and fidelity, of selfless commitment for freedom and justice in society, may sound much more secular than your theologians now might like to hear. But I stress the point stubbornly: these sorts of indoctrinations and commands from outside, these channels of grace from outside are only of any use if they meet the ultimate grace that comes from within. That was the lesson of my own experience once I first made my own "Exercises" in Manresa, when the eyes of my spirit were opened, and everything could be seen within God's own self. This realization I wanted to pass on to others through the Exercises that I gave.

It seems to me obvious that this kind of help in watering the ground, help toward an immediate encounter with God (or should we say toward the realization that the human person is always in a state of having already met God, and is continuing to do so?), is more important today than ever. Without this we couldn't avoid the danger of all the theology lessons and all the moral directives getting swallowed up in the deadly silence that today's atheism — without people noticing that this terrible silence is still speaking of God — spreads over just everyone. Again — I keep on saying this — I can't give Exercises now, and so of course my assurance that a person can meet God immediately is an unverified promise. But do you understand me now when I say that the central task for you Jesuits, around which everything else is centered, has to be the giving of the Exercises?

Of course this doesn't mean beginning with official and organized ecclesiastical courses, given to many people at once — still less is that the main point. Rather it means *mystagogical* help, so that others don't repress God's immediacy but come to experience it clearly and accept it. This doesn't mean that all of you can or should give the Exercises in this formal sense; there's no need for all of you to talk yourselves into thinking you can do it. I'm also not devaluing all the other pastoral, academic, and political enterprises that you've thought you needed to try in the course of your history. But all this other stuff should really be understood as a preparation for this ultimate task or as following on from it, a task that must remain yours in the future: that of helping people toward the immediate experience of God, the experience where it dawns on human beings that the mystery all grasp that we call God is near, can be spoken to, and enfolds us with blessing precisely when we don't try to make it something under our control, but hand ourselves over to it unconditionally. Everything you do you should be constantly testing to see if it serves this goal.

— "Ignatius of Loyola Speaks to a Modern Jesuit," 15–16

Rahner's theology and spirituality affirm the human: we find God by appropriating, rather than shunning, our everyday experience. But this in no way means that Rahner makes light of human fragility; indeed, one of the fruits of a mature spirituality is an ability to face limitation in freedom, secure in the gospel truth that God, in Christ, has shown how all that is human lies enfolded within the divine compassion. In Lent 1946, Rahner preached a series of sermons on prayer in downtown Munich. The ruins of the magnificent baroque church all too powerfully symbolized the degradation of Nazism, and wartime experience supplied vivid imagery:

> Do you remember the nights in the cellar, the nights of deadly loneliness amid the harrowing crush of people? The nights of helplessness, of waiting for a meaningless death? The nights with the lights going out, and horror and powerlessness gripping our hearts? When we're just playing at being brave and relaxed? When our own easy pleasantries and brave expressions sound so strangely wooden and empty and seem to have died on us even before they've reached the other person? When we just give up, when we are keeping quiet, when we are just waiting without hope for the end, for death? Alone, powerless, empty.

Rahner then extends the image: imagine that the cellar is blocked up, permanently: "then we've got a perfect image for humanity today." It is precisely in this limited, frustrated humanity that "God is to be found. God is not in any simple sense our rescuer, but rather the one who is present with us, precisely in our sense of guilt and limitation. Our task is to accept ourselves, and the God present with us, in trust."

OPENING THE HEART

Is it hopeless, the situation of the blocked-up heart? Is the danger of collapse and of inner suffocation unavoidable? What are people to do if they are to manage an escape from the dungeon of the cold despair and disappointment that they disguise? How

does the heart's opening take place? We can say it in a word: in
prayer, prayer to God, just in prayer. But because we're still trying to understand what "prayer" means, we need to go slowly
and talk cautiously. Let's ask what people need to do when they
find themselves in this situation with their hearts blocked up.

The first thing is this. They must just stay there and let go.
When people notice that in fact their souls are blocked up, they
either begin to defend themselves with the desperation of a person drowning, indeed of a person being buried alive — plunging
into everything, into every form of activity and busyness that
gives them hope of fooling themselves about their despair. Or
else they really despair: either in overt frenzy or else quietly
and icily they curse, they hate themselves and the world, and
they say there is no God. They say there is no God because
they are confusing the true God with what they took to be their
God. And as regards what they are actually referring to, they
are quite right. The God they were referring to really does not
exist: the God of earthly security, the God of salvation from
life's disappointments, the God of life insurance, the God who
takes care so that children never cry and that justice marches
in upon the earth, the God who transforms earth's laments, the
God who doesn't let human love end up in disappointment.

But like the first group, this second sort of person cannot in
fact remain in despair. They think they have courageously and
honestly drawn the right conclusion from their life-experience,
but they haven't really understood despair, because they have
seen in it God's death rather than God's true advent. No, the
real truth is that in this event of the heart you can happily let
despair seem to take away everything from you, but in truth
it's only what is finite and null that is taken, no matter how
great and wonderful it was, no matter indeed if it's your very
self — you yourself with your ideals; you yourself with your life-
projects, all so very cleverly, so very precisely, so very nicely set
out; you with your image of God, the image that was like you

rather than like the Self of the One past all grasp. What can be taken from you is never God. Even if all your exits are barred, it's only the exits into what is finite that are blocked, the exits into what really are dead ends. Don't be shocked at the loneliness and desertedness of your inner prison, which seems to be filled only with powerlessness and hopelessness, with tiredness and emptiness! Don't be shocked.

For look, if you stand firm, if you don't run away from despair, if in your despair at the idols of your life up till now, idols of body or mind, beautiful and honorable idols (for yes, they are beautiful and honorable), idols that you called God — if in this despair you don't despair of the true God, if you can stand firm in this way (this is already a miracle of grace, but it's there for you) then you will suddenly become aware that you're not in fact buried alive at all, that your prison is shutting you off only from what is null and finite, that its deathly emptiness is only a disguise for an intimacy of God's, that God's silence, the eerie stillness, is filled by the Word without words, by Him who is above all names, by Him who is all in all. And his silence is telling you that He is here.

And this is the second thing you should do in your despair: notice that He is here, know that He is with you. Be aware that for a long time He has been waiting for you in the deepest dungeon of your blocked-up heart. Be aware that He has been listening for a long time, to see if you — after all the busy noise of your life, all the talk that you call your "illusion-free philosophy" or perhaps even your prayer, noise and talk in which you are only talking to yourself, after all the despairing, weeping and silent sighing over the need in your life — He has been listening to see if you might finally be able to be silent before Him and let Him have the word, the word that appears to the person you were up till now only as a deathly silence.

When you give up your frantic, violent inner anxiety about yourself and your life, your feeling should not be that you are in any way falling; when you doubt yourself, your wisdom, your strength, your capacity to make life and the happiness that comes from freedom for yourself, you should not despair. Rather, you should feel you are with Him, suddenly, as through a miracle that must happen every day anew and that can never become routine. You will suddenly realize that the petrifying face of despair is only God's rising in your soul, that the darkness of the world is nothing but the shadowless radiance of God, that what seems a dead end with no way out is only the immensity of God, God who needs no ways because He is already here.

Then you will notice that He doesn't actually need to come into your blocked up heart — rather you just have to understand that you shouldn't try to run away from this heart, because He is here after all, and thus there can be no reason to flee from this blessed desperation toward a consolation that would be false and that doesn't exist. Then you will notice that you — this is the free "yes" of your faith and your love — have to turn and enter into this blocked-up heart in order to find there the One who was always there already, waiting, the true and living God. That, then, is the second thing. He is there. He is right within your blocked-up heart. He alone. He, however, who is all, and therefore looks as though He is nothing. He is there because of — not despite — your having nothing else any more, not even yourself.

— *The Need and the Blessing of Prayer,* 7–9

What Rahner describes here, accepting oneself and accepting God, is the task of a lifetime. People appropriate their experience, limited and particular as it is, as sustained by an unbounded, self-giving God, in different ways and to differing extents.[3] *Two general points nevertheless remain valid. The first*

---

3. When Rahner handles the theme in *Foundations of Christian Faith,* 59, he writes as follows: "those experiences in which the individual in his or her individuality

is that moments of suffering have a particular significance. In this context, Rahner's language sometimes contrasts the life of God and the life of the world; but in fact he is only taking his vision of God's presence in the creation to its logical conclusion. For only the experience of finding God in dark places, in situations that any secular ideology of progress can only dismiss as meaningless, can assure us — in the words of the next extract — that we are not simply mixing up Christianity with "ourselves and our own life impulse."

"On the Experience of Grace," first published in 1954, was a favorite piece of Rahner's. What it says about negative experiences and their special significance in the Christian life parallels once again the teaching of Ignatius. Christ's cross is important for our decision-making, not because there is any religious value in the unpleasant as such, but because good decisions — which may well be for what we find most congenial — should be informed by a passionate desire for the God who mysteriously brings good out of evil.

ON THE EXPERIENCE OF GRACE

Have we ever once actually had the experience of grace? We don't mean by that any old pious feeling, or the religious uplift one might get on a feast day, or a gentle sense of comfort, but simply the experience of grace — the experience of the visitation of the Holy Spirit of the triune God, the visitation that has become actual with Christ, through his Incarnation and through his sacrifice on the cross. Can one experience grace in this life at all? If we say yes, doesn't this destroy faith, that cloud of

---

had the experience of transcendence and of being taken up out of themselves into the ineffable mystery. . . . [T]he clarity and persuasiveness of the various individual experiences of this kind . . . vary a great deal in individual persons, . . . (and the process of appropriating them) . . . would have to vary a great deal from person to person. . . . [It] is possible for the individual only in individual conversation and quasi-therapy."

bright darkness that enwraps us as long as we are making our pilgrimage here on earth? Now of course the mystics say — and they would attest to the truth of their statement by laying down their lives — that they have already experienced God, and thus also grace. But this experiential knowledge of God in mysticism is a dark and mysterious business; one cannot talk about it if one has not had it, and one does not talk about it if one has. So our question does not admit of a simple answer straight off.

But are there perhaps steps in the experience of grace, with the lowest ones accessible to us too? Let's ask ourselves first: have we ever experienced what makes a human person a spirit? (What "spirit" refers to here is itself a difficult question that cannot be given a one-word answer.) Perhaps we will answer: "Of course I have had this experience — I have it every day, all the time. I think; I study; I make decisions; I do things; I cultivate relationships with other people; I live in a society based not just on physical factors but also on the mind and heart; I love; I enjoy myself; I appreciate poetry; I am endowed with the riches coming from culture, from scholarship, from art, and so on. So I know what 'spirit' is."

But it is not as simple as that. Of course all that is true. But in all the realities just named, "spirit" is — or can be — just an extra something, so to speak, serving to make this earthly life humane, pleasant, somehow meaningful. In all that, there is no necessity for us to have experienced what really makes the spirit transcendent. Now, this is not to say that the spirit as such is present only when people are talking and philosophizing about the spirit's transcendence. On the contrary. That would be only a derived, secondary experience of this spirit (for the spirit isn't confined to being just an interior aspect of humanity's life). But where is the experience of the spirit in the proper sense? Now we can begin to say: "Let's try to discover it ourselves, in our experience." And now we can perhaps point to a few things, just diffidently and cautiously.

Have we ever once remained silent, though we wanted to defend ourselves, though we were treated unfairly? Have we ever once forgiven, though we received no reward for it and people took it for granted. Have we ever once obeyed, not because we had to or else we'd have had unpleasantness, but simply because of that mysterious, silent, unfathomable reality we call God and God's will? Have we ever once made a sacrifice, without thanks, without recognition, even without a feeling of satisfaction inside? Have we ever once been absolutely lonely? Have we ever once made up our mind to do something purely on the basis of our conscience's innermost judgment, from a place beyond where anyone can express it or describe it, a place where you are quite alone, and where you know you are making a decision that no one will take away from you and for which the responsibility will be yours, always and eternally? Have we ever once tried to love God in a place where no wave of felt enthusiasm is carrying us along anymore, where we can no longer mix up ourselves and our own life impulse with God — a place where we think that this kind of love is killing us, where this love looks like death and absolute negativity, a place where we seem to be calling into the void, into something unspeakable, a place where it looks like a terrible leap into a bottomless expanse, a place where everything seems to be getting out of control and ceasing — so it seems — to make sense? Have we ever done our duty in a situation where it seems that we can do it only with a burning feeling of negating and obliterating our very self, when it seems that we are doing something terribly stupid for which no one is going to thank us? Have we ever once been good to someone from whom no echo of gratitude or comprehension comes back, and neither were we rewarded with the feeling of having been "selfless," decent, or the like?

Let's look, ourselves, within this kind of life-experience, let's look for our own experiences where something just like this has happened to us. If we find this sort of thing, then we've had the experience of the Spirit that is meant here. The experience of eternity, the experience that the Spirit is more than a piece of this temporal world, the experience that humanity's meaning is not commensurate with this world's meaning and fortune, the experience of risk, of trustfully taking the plunge in a way that in fact has no visible justification in terms derived from this world's success.

From this standpoint, we might be able to understand the kind of secret passion that lives in real people of the Spirit and in saints. They want to have this experience; they want to assure themselves, in their secret fear of being stuck in the world, that they are beginning to live in the Spirit. They have caught the taste of the spirit. Average people just see experiences like these as unpleasant, if not fully avoidable, interruptions of a proper, normal life; for them, spirit is just a seasoning and decoration of life that is in itself not-spirit; for them spirit is not the central thing. But people of the Spirit and saints have acquired the taste for the pure spirit. In a certain way, they drink the spirit straight — they do not just enjoy it as a seasoning to earthly existence. That is why they live in a strange way, why they are poor, why they yearn for humility, why they long for death, why they are ready to suffer, why they have a secret longing for martyrdom.

It is not as though they are not also weak. It is not as though they must not always be turning back into normal everyday life. It is not as though they do not know that grace can also bless everyday reality, can bless commonsense actions, and can transform these too into a step toward God. It is not as though they don't know that we here aren't angels, nor are we meant to be. But they know that the human person is spirit, and as such should live — really live, not just speculate about it — at the boundary between God and world, time and eternity. And they are always seeking to assure themselves that they are really doing this, and that the spirit within them is not just a way of making life humane.

Now, if we have this kind of experience of the spirit, then in actual fact we (at least we Christians who live in faith) have already had an experience of the supernatural.[4] Very anonymously, implicitly perhaps. Probably indeed in such a way that we can't, indeed mustn't turn round so as to look the supernatural direct in the face. But if we abandon ourselves in this experience of the spirit; if what can be grasped and stated, what can be enjoyed founders; if it all sounds like deadly silence, or it all disappears into an unnameable, so to speak blank and colorless, inapprehensible blessedness — then we know that in actual fact it is not just the spirit but the Holy Spirit that is at work. Then it is the hour of the Spirit's grace. Then what seems the unspeakable sense that our existence has no ground — *that* is the ungroundedness of God, communicating God's self to us: God's endlessness is beginning to come, an endlessness where there are no longer paths, and that tastes like a Nothing because it is endless. When we have let go and no longer belong to ourselves, when we have denied ourselves and no longer have control over ourselves, when everything, and our very selves with it, has been pushed back away from us as if into an infinite distance — then we are beginning to live in the world of God's self, of the God of grace and eternal life.

At the beginning it may still seem strange to us, and we will always be getting tempted to flee back in fear to what is familiar and close — indeed we will often have to do this, and be allowed to do this. Nevertheless we should gradually accustom ourselves to the taste of the pure wine of the spirit, which is filled with the Holy Spirit. At least enough that we don't push

---

4. In Rahner's theology "supernatural" is a technical word. It has nothing to do with the paranormal. It denotes that aspect of God's presence to us that depends only on *grace*, on God's existing for us as *self*-giver — as opposed to the natural, which could be deduced from God's activity as Creator.

the chalice away when God's guidance and providence hands
it to us.

The chalice of the Holy Spirit is identical in this life with the
chalice of Christ. But only those can drink it who have slowly
learned a little about tasting fullness out of emptiness, rising out
of setting, life out of death, finding out of renunciation. People
who are learning this are having the experience of the spirit, the
pure spirit — and in this experience they are experiencing the
Holy Spirit of grace. For you can come to this liberation of the
spirit in a full and lasting way only through the grace of Christ
in faith. Conversely, where he liberates this spirit, he liberates it
into the life of God's own self, through supernatural grace.

Let us ponder our own lives and look for our own experience
of grace. Not so as to say: "there it is, I've got it." You cannot
find it in such a way as to claim it in triumph as your property
and possession. You can look for it only by forgetting yourself;
you can find it only by seeking God and handing yourself over
to God in self-forgetting love, without still, as it were, trying
to go back on it. But you should every so often ask yourself
if something like this death-dealing, life-bringing experience is
alive in you, so that you can realize how far the road still is, and
how far distant away from the experience of the Holy Spirit we
are living in our so-called "spiritual life." *Grandis nobis restat
via; venite et gustate quam suavis sit Dominus!* There is still a
long way lying before us. Come and taste, how rich in love the
Lord is!   — *Theological Investigations,* 3:86–90

*"I was not playing at love," a medieval mystic once heard
Christ saying. The grace of God extends into the bleakest and
most painful depths of the human, even if the resurrection
assures us that this is good news, that bleakness is not the
end of the story. But though our experience of grace is somehow fixed and assured by the memory of Christ crucified and
risen, each of us appropriates this grace in a different way. We*

discover this way as we make our life-choices. Those well so-
cialized into Churches might want to call the process "spiritual
discernment," and Rahner himself connects it to his deepest
convictions about how God relates to the world. But the pro-
cess often occurs, and occurs healthily, without our necessarily
naming it for what it is.

SPIRITUAL CHOICES

When I say that one can meet God immediately in your time
too, just like in mine, I mean really God, the God past all grasp,
the mystery beyond speech, the darkness that is light only to
those who let themselves be swallowed by it unconditionally,
the God who is now beyond all names. But equally it was just
this God, no other, that I experienced as the God who descends
to us, who comes near to us, in whose incomprehensible fire we
do not in fact burn up, but rather come to be for the first time,
and are eternally affirmed. The God beyond speech speaks Himself to us; in this speaking of His unspeakableness we come to
be, we live, we are loved, we are affirmed; if we let ourselves be
taken by God, we are not annihilated by God; rather, we receive
our existence for the first time. The empty creation becomes infinitely important, ineffably great and beautiful, because it is
gifted by God with God's own self.

Without God, we would be erring all over the realm of our
freedom and our decisions, always insecure, and in the end
desperately bored. For anything we might choose is ultimately
finite; it can always be superseded by something else, and thus
it makes no real difference. I, however, came to experience that
in the realm of this freedom of mine with its possibilities the
infinitely free God could still surround one thing rather than
another with His special love, and let it, unlike other things, be

transparent to His own self, so that this thing was not obscuring God, but rather letting God be loved in itself, and letting itself be loved in God — thus showing itself as "God's will."

When I used to envisage and play out to myself my freedom's possibilities, and set them before my freedom's emerging decision, I experienced that, on the one hand, one alternative shone through itself, fitted into the open freedom that leads to God's own self and remained transparent to Him, whereas this was not the case with the other — though, in themselves, all such possibilities, which, each in their own way, derive from God, could have been small tokens of the infinite God. In some way like this (it's difficult to make it clear) I learned to make further distinctions within what was already seen as objectively and rationally possible and as ecclesiastically permissible: distinctions between that bounded reality in which the incomprehensibility of the boundless God willed to be near me, and that in which, although a matter of empirical fact and in itself also quite sensible, remained in a certain way dark and an obstruction to God. It would, after all, be crazy just to say that everything in reality — just on the ground that it is real and originates in God — must offer equal access to God for every human individual. For then no decision of our freedom, even unavoidable ones, would have any special significance.

What I have just said, however, does not fully name this experience of God's "incarnation" in God's creature — an experience in which it is not that the creature is obliterated the nearer it comes to God, but rather becomes properly established for the first time. The person who, in this way, has come immediately before God participates, so to speak — however much this might seem beyond our understanding — in God's action of descent into finitude, the finitude that thus becomes good. God may be nameless, unfathomable, unmanipulable, incalculable — but that must not mean that God vanishes out of sight from the one praying and acting. God must not become the sun that makes everything visible and itself remains unseen. God must remain in immediacy and must hold everything else fast in its finitude and relativity with — as I would almost like to say — merciless clarity. But it is in just this merciless light that what is preferred by God's self-giving love appears *as* that: what is loved, what is preferred, what has been chosen to be from among many other possibilities remaining empty. And the human person, standing in God's modeless light, itself comes to take part in this inclining action of God toward a particular, finite creature; they can take this finite really seriously; the creature itself is for the person lovable, beautiful, ultimately of eternal validity, because God's own self can accomplish and does accomplish the past-all-grasp miracle of His love, that of giving Himself.

When participating like this in God's inclining, God's descent into what is finite — which God does without self-diminishment and without burning up this finite reality — a human person can no longer be the one whose deepest-down torment and desire alike is to lay bare the relativity and meaninglessness of everything and anything, the one who either idolizes or (ultimately) makes a nothing of a distinct finite reality. This experience of becoming part of God's inclining to what is not God, and yet which, without there being any confusion, can no longer, as a result of this inclining, be separated from God,[5] is first had when one thing is experienced as willed by God in contrast to another. But since this other to which God inclines is, in practice and when you look at it truly, the human person who is our neighbor, not a thing, this participating in God's inclining is the true love of neighbor, about which I will have to speak more

---

5. Rahner is echoing here the teaching of the Council of Chalcedon. The divine and human natures of Christ "undergo no confusion...no separation." Rahner's point is that the structure of reality manifested in Christ must also be reflected in the creation as a whole. We thus discover and appropriate our full identity under God in and through the discovery of this pattern in our human possibilities.

explicitly later. The love of God, which seems as if it allows the world to be suppressed, is in fact a love for the world that loves the world with God, and thus allows the world to rise eternally.

— "Ignatius of Loyola Speaks to a Modern Jesuit," 17–18

For Rahner, then, we discover God by recognizing how particular options in our lives are somehow our right way toward God. The text that follows, a late essay written in 1973 for the eightieth birthday of his colleague Johannes Baptist Lotz, sets out more fully the theology behind this conviction. It begins with a demolition of most rationales given for petitionary prayer, and indeed for the idea of prayer as any kind of conversation between the creature and God. Instead it insists that the "conversation" in question must be of a quite unique kind, one in which we creatures experience ourselves as the word of God. When we are in touch with this fundamental reality, then we can also experience harmonies and disharmonies between it and the particular options we envisage for ourselves.

COLLOQUY WITH GOD?

Anyone who reads Christian spiritual literature, anyone who listens to sermons on prayer, will be familiar with the statement that prayer is a "dialogue with God." There is certainly no need to gather together here examples of this commonplace of Christian spirituality and of the theology of prayer. Perhaps, however, it is not completely pointless to offer some reflections on the question of whether and in what sense prayer can be called a dialogue with God. For, after all, this word "dialogue" presupposes that in prayer it is not just humanity but God's own self that speaks, speaks to us, speaks in such a way as to answer our words. The question that is to occupy us here is thus not the more general and comprehensive question about whether prayer is possible at all, and what preconditions it must have, in other words the question of the personal address that a human being can direct to God (today, certainly, not an easy problem). Rather we are asking whether, and in what sense, we can say that in prayer God speaks to humanity in such a way that we can really call prayer a dialogue between God and humanity.

Certainly, human beings today have great difficulty in understanding and recognizing that in prayer they experience something like God's personally speaking. In this kind of short essay we can justifiably leave aside the wider questions about a personal experience of God as existing and the God-humanity, God-world relationship — questions that are already quite difficult enough for human beings today. But apart from these, the specific difficulty with experiencing prayer as dialogue is this: our first inclination is to take as the person's own mental state or activity what a more exuberant piety is accustomed or inclined to interpret as God's speaking to us.

The point is undoubtedly correct; it must not be denied; and these days we cannot naively ignore it. The question then arises: why can this be understood as a special manifestation of God, as God's speaking? People today have the impression that in prayer they are to a certain extent talking and deliberating with themselves — with this talking to oneself perhaps being about God, this self-reflection perhaps happening "before" God. If they experience particular sudden, unexpected, strong inbreakings or outbreakings of new ideas and impulses (of course this happens), people today will initially interpret such occurrences as things happening within their own existence, as the deeper levels of the soul expressing themselves, as the breakthrough of what was previously repressed, as a fortunate interplay of subconscious associations, or the like. They will point to the fact that the same somewhat out of the ordinary mental processes are also present where there is no question of specifically religious content: with artistic intuitions and ideas that cannot in any real sense be programmed in advance, in sudden transformations of the whole person that are not expressly motivated by religion, and so on.

There is no need here to investigate whether this is right or not quite right; be that as it may, people today have the impression that it would be to accept the miraculous, or else old-fashioned mythology, if they were to understand an unexpected, powerful mental event, just because it was sudden, vivid, and significant, as resulting from an intervention of God at a particular point in space and time within the normal course of their mental history. In the mental sphere, at least generally speaking, this appears to people today just as improbable and incredible as miracles in the external sphere (understood as new interventions of God in God's world). People today, even if they recognize God's existence, explain the course of their inner world in terms of causes within the world. And these remain causes within the world, even if they produce less normal phenomena within the sphere of consciousness.

Of course there are still also today many people in the Church, especially in the many groups with a charismatic piety, who understand specific mental experiences, especially speaking in tongues, baptism in the Spirit, radical conversion and the like, quite uninhibitedly as charismatic interventions of the Holy Spirit "from outside." They more or less ignore the simple fact that all such experiences are, to begin with, *theirs;* at least until the contrary is strictly proven — something not the case even with parapsychological phenomena — they must be explained as the effects of states of affairs, external and internal, present within themselves. Moreover, an outsider can see parallels to all such charismatic phenomena in non-Christian religions, which clearly display all these mental causes — the nature, the style of consciousness, the language, the limitations — with the result that this alone makes it almost impossible to discover or look for anything that must necessarily be traced back to a special, miraculous intervention of God. On these and similar grounds, people today find it very difficult to discover something in their praying consciousness that they want to interpret simply as God speaking as opposed to themselves speaking. Prayer seems to them to be a monologue, or at best talking to oneself, but not a dialogue with God, not an event that one could seriously call, seriously and without too much reservation, dialogue. [...]

There follows a technical passage, in which Rahner shows up as inadequate various strategies adopted in the history of theology and of spirituality to deal with the problem.

People often, presumably as a way of making the question easier, begin by taking it as a given that God is a person, and on that basis conclude that God can be spoken to by us. Once you have got that far, you have the idea that you are already standing in a relationship of dialogue, which can be brought to life without further ado. But even if you can take it for granted that God can, objectively, be thought of as "personal," this does not yet give justification for the two further steps needed before one is really in dialogue with God. It is still not clear that the personal God can be talked to by us; and, most important of all and even if that last point were granted, it needs to be made clearer how it is that God answers such talk, and does not stay silent.[...]

It is in another way that we must try to move forward. So far our reflections about prayer as dialogue with God have just assumed that in prayer there is "something" that God says to us. We were assuming in setting up the problem that what constitutes something like a dialogue with God is one element among others in our consciousness, a particular, single, identifiable element, immediately caused by God in a particular, distinctive

way, and recognized as caused in this way. And the difficulties we have been talking about so far were brought along by
this assumption. But what would it be like if we were to say, if
we were able to say, this: in prayer, we experience *ourselves* as
what God has spoken, as arising in the specificity of our existence from God's sovereign freedom, and as at God's disposal.
What would it be like if we were to say: it is *we ourselves* who
are what God first says to us, in the way our freedom is defined,
in the way our future is indefinite, in the sheer facts of our past
and present that can never be fully explained away by a theory,
never given a rationale in terms of the purpose they serve?

If *this* is how we understand the question informing all these
reflections of ours, then this implies right from the start that the
relationship of "partnership" and "dialogue" between God and
us is of a kind that is quite unique. It cannot be compared with
other such relationships. It must not be simply thought of as a
partnership in the same sense as a relationship of partnership
and dialogue between human beings. And just this much will be
quite enough, of course, for the idea of "dialogue" — when it is
meant to designate a particular characteristic of prayer — also
to be understood in a unique way that cannot be compared with
other instances. If we can answer the question asked just now
with a yes, then *we ourselves* (in our transcendence, which experiences itself as such as coming from elsewhere, as we might
say) are the expression and speech of God, listening to itself.

But this must not be understood merely as a general principle; it is a statement about the quite specific ways we live our
lives, particularly, uniquely, historically — lived lives that we experience as given to us, and thus spoken by God to Himself.
God's most primordial word to us in our free uniqueness is not
a word that occurs identifiably, as a point within the broader
sphere of our consciousness, as something added on, as one object of experience alongside others. Rather, it is *ourselves,* in
our unity, totality, and dependence on the mystery past all grasp

that we call God — it is the Word of God that *we ourselves* are, and that is spoken to us as such.

These sentences seem to sound like merely a matter of existentialist philosophy. But when we read them with the assumption that this transcendence is always, everywhere (because of God's will that all should be saved) raised and radicalized to God's immediacy by what we call supernatural grace, the self-communication of God, then such sentences are directly theological. If human beings experience themselves — in the unity of grace and their spirit — as what God speaks to God's own self (and this as their distinctive identity, which as it is lived out specifically also involves God's free, self-imparting grace); and if they in prayer admit and freely accept this lived reality as God's Word, a Word in which God is speaking Himself to humanity, then prayer is already (in an initial sense that we still need to fill out below) dialogical, a dialogue with God. Human beings hear *themselves* as God's speaking, filled by faith, hope, and love with God's self-expression in gracious self-communication. They do not hear "something" over and above themselves, as if they were already there as a brute fact; they hear *themselves* as the word spoken, the word in which God constitutes a hearer, and to which He speaks Himself as answer. [...]

But with this we have named only one aspect of prayer, the "transcendental" aspect: this makes intelligible the idea of prayer as dialogue in a quite special sense. We must add a second sense: this sense gives real grounding to the conventional understanding of prayer as dialogue, as well as purifying this of mythological misunderstandings in terms of the miraculous. For when human beings accept, unconditionally and unobstructedly, this absolute openness for God that comes from God and God's freedom, and is the primordial word of God to humanity; when this is not blocked, distorted, or taken in vain by a free human preference for quite particular, identifiable contents in their consciousness, then we have (if I may be allowed what perhaps seems an arbitrary leap of thought) what Ignatius of Loyola in the Exercises calls "indifference," and (if this indifference is really enacted in radical freedom and sustained) "consolation without preceding cause."

Now one may encounter a particular, single object of choice within this kind of ultimate dialogical freedom, an object that does not block, confuse or restrict — even after relatively long spiritual experience and examination — this pure openness to God; on the contrary, it is experienced as the mediation through which we can accept and maintain this indifferent openness to God in unconditional self-surrender to Him, or (to put it the other way round) in the unconditional acceptance of the Word of God that we ourselves are. In this case, this identifiable object of choice (however much it itself might be something within the world and relative) can be legitimately understood as an episode in this dialogical relationship between God and humanity, because, and insofar as, this object of choice fits within the whole of this dialogical conversation, without endangering or suppressing its absolute, unconditional openness.

Seen as a thing in itself — purely within the world and categorically — this kind of categorical object of choice that a person decides for in prayer can always be problematic; perhaps it will prove later to be, when measured against human needs and structures, inadequate, provisional, replaceable, even harmful. Nevertheless, it was then and there the best mediation of this indifferent, transcendental openness where humanity experiences *itself* as the expressed Word of God, and therefore as the salvific will of God. In this sort of logic of existential knowledge and freedom, prayer then becomes dialogical as regards its individual, identifiable content too. It is not that we are understanding just anything that turns up in consciousness with a certain surprising suddenness or unexpectedness, or with a sentimental emotion, as for that reason alone a working of the Spirit, and therefore as God's speaking — a claim that would then need to be played up fervently against a straightforward, skeptical psychology. The point is different: when the particular reality in consciousness that we decide for can stand within a permanent and unconditional openness to God (we could also say "within an absolute critical freedom") positively as its mediation, then this kind of particular reality can count as spoken by God to us, in and alongside that fundamental speaking of God to us that we ourselves are and that in prayer we hear and accept.

I am not claiming here that these two points that I have tried very briefly to indicate constitute the dialogical character of prayer in its entirety. I will be content if it can be agreed that I have done at least something to clarify the dialogical character of prayer. Of course too, it is impossible to explain any further consequences of this kind of understanding of prayer as a dialogue. Perhaps now it seems more difficult than one normally thinks to understand prayer seriously and realistically as a dialogue with God, and in particular to experience it in practice, now that it has been "demythologized," as dialogue. But there was never any intention to say that normal believers in their spontaneous everyday life need to have all the ideas expressed here at the forefront of their minds. Once they have gone through this kind of reflection and lost their illusions, they can have a kind of second naiveté about prayer as dialogue with God. Because dialogue is what prayer truly is.

— *Theological Investigations,* 18:122–31

Writing in 1973, and honoring a colleague who was a distinguished philosopher, Rahner used abstract, philosophical language. But behind it lay human realities. One of the earliest of his writings on decision is a sermon preached to young Jesuits during World War II in Vienna, where they were studying

theology between spells in the Nazi forces. Stanislaus Kotzka,
a young Pole from a noble family, who was studying in the
Jesuit college in Vienna, had decided in 1567 to join the new Je-
suit order. The resistance of his family, and indeed of the Jesuit
community — who had no wish to offend his family — led him
eventually simply to walk first to Germany and then to Rome
in order to present himself. He died of malaria in the novitiate
after a year. The room where he allegedly made his decision
was a shrine, and Mass would be said there on his feast day for
the Jesuit students. In the situation of wartime, when the Nazis
would almost certainly have exterminated the Jesuits had they
won, Rahner's reflections on decision and commitment take on
added poignancy.

STANISLAUS KOTZKA

We have come together here to offer to God the Father the
sacrifice of the new and everlasting covenant on the feast of
St. Stanislaus. We are where Stanislaus set out on the way of
life that is also ours, and that led him to God.

In this room, he came to the decision to leave Vienna and to
find the Society of Jesus in whatever way and at whatever cost.
It was from here that he began the decisive stage of his life, his
final stage. Thus here was a place where he made an unambiguous decision to take firm responsibility for himself, a place of
decision to make a sacrifice, a place of decision for brotherly
community.

Here is a place where he made an unambiguous decision to
take firm responsibility for himself. Stanislaus had to decide on
his path alone. The decision he took had no one else to support
it — there was no one else to ask, no one else onto whom he
might have unloaded his responsibility. The people around him
were against it. Quite unequivocally against it. The Jesuits, then

as now, were very cautious and reserved and didn't want anything to do with the matter. And of course prudence is a virtue.
But not the only one we have to consider. The decision he made
looked desperately like a young man's silly exploit, like a mixture of pious exaltation and childish naiveté. But I cannot think
that Stanislaus was so childish — when one has consciously
looked death in the face as he had, childishness stops — or that
he was not conscious of how his decision was "impossible,"
"vulgar." But he made his decision against the people around
him, against so-called common sense, and despite the caution
of the Jesuits regarding the risk he was taking.

And he was right. Right, because in this decision he was not
seeking himself but God, and because he had the toughness and
strength to carry the decision through to the end and to bear all
the consequences. This room is a place where he made an unambiguous decision to take firm responsibility for himself. And
Stanislaus stands before us as an example with a message. Inevitably, life as a scholastic[6] is always one great temptation to
avoid taking serious responsibility for one's own life. You don't
have to worry about the practical things in life — that's still true
today to a large extent. [...] You have the sense of having done
your duty if you avoid conflict with superiors and examiners, or
at least evoke the impression of having done your work, as carefully and caringly assigned from above. Let us ask ourselves in
this room if we feel the courage and the duty to take responsibility for ourselves. Could we too ever demand of ourselves an
action, a piece of work, a struggle to find something out, even
if no one around us believes in it, and perhaps many are against
it? If we no longer feel that, in the end, it is we ourselves who
alone are responsible for our lives, and that this responsibility

---

6. Jesuit jargon for the stages between novitiate and final profession, often used
less correctly to refer only to Jesuit priest students prior to their ordination (which
typically takes place before final profession).

is a serious, indeed *the* serious concern of our lives before God, then we are no true companions of this saint.

Here is a place of decision for making a sacrifice. The decision Stanislaus made, judged by worldly and secular standards (and we always judge that way), was a very insignificant, laughable, deplorable business. For the unbeliever hidden within *us,* how laughable can it, must it appear when a young man decides for a poorer, more constrained life. When Stanislaus felt he had to go off to a committed life (which made his brother — who also, without doubt, claimed to be a "good Catholic" — furious, very understandably when he had to look at these "hysterical" goings on), he obviously saw behind this life something that not everyone sees. Only people of faith see it: those whom Christ calls blessed on account of this insight and of what they thus do, those who know that Christ's cross, folly and scandal, is God's wisdom and God's power. Let us not indulge in false heroics. Nevertheless, this place of Stanislaus's decision, this moment when we celebrate the memorial of the Lord's death — this is the time and place to pray God once again that when the sacrifice to which we have pledged ourselves touches us in our hearts, as it must, differently from how we expected it, we can say yes — as a matter of course, without fuss, and yet in faith and with gladness.

Here is a place of decision for brotherly community, because it was from here that Stanislaus saw his way into the Society of Jesus. His acquaintance with the Fathers in Vienna had obviously not frightened him off, although one can hardly assume that these experiences were in all respects simply enjoyable. And thus his decision was also a decision for brotherly community. He had friends in the Society. His fellow novice, who had the task of teaching him Italian, became his good friend, and Stanislaus told him about himself. And Claudio Acquaviva[7] was

---

7. General Superior of the Jesuits between 1590 and 1615.

proud even forty years later of his special friendship with the saint in the novitiate. He was a good companion to all. We live today under conditions that make brotherly community difficult and that require new forms to be found. Let us look for these ourselves, and not wait for decrees from on high. Let us be true friends and comrades who help each other, who do things together, who try to serve each other, who even now are planning work together for the future.

We are celebrating the sacrifice of Christ, and its reality among us now of the great decision on which the world's salvation depended, of the absolute sacrifice, of the deed of love, of the sacrament of human beings in loving union with each other. We are celebrating it in the room of a person's decision to take firm responsibility for himself, a decision for making sacrifice, a decision for brotherly community. May God give us the grace to understand the meaning of this moment a little more deeply.

— "Homily for the Feast of St. Stanislaus,"
unpublished, Karl-Rahner Archiv, 1.C.48[8]

---

8. No critical edition of this text has yet been made, though one should appear in due course in *Karl Rahner Sämtliche Werke*. Rahner's notes are hard to read and, of course, may themselves include errors. This translation makes a few tacit assumptions.

3

Jesus

But now I must speak of Jesus. Perhaps it seemed, in all I have said up till now, as if I had forgotten Jesus and his blessed Name? Not so: he was present implicitly in all I have said.... [1]

In his "spiritual testament," Rahner names Jesus relatively late, only after he has written at length about God's presence in human experience at large.

For me in my day it was no problem to find God in Jesus and Jesus in God (or at least only the problem of how to love him and how to follow him truly). God uniquely in him.

It was just that he had good reasons for not talking about Jesus too early.

Christian tradition gives us two statements that, on the surface, can seem contradictory. "I am the Way, and the Truth, and the Life. No one comes to the Father except through me," says the Jesus of the Fourth Gospel (John 14:6). It is natural to read those sentences as making an exclusive claim, a claim that only through Jesus can we find the goodness of God, and

---

1. "Ignatius of Loyola Speaks to a Modern Jesuit," 19–20.

*a claim that whatever lies outside Jesus' influence is somehow
outside the care of God. But against this way of thinking, we
need to set Christianity's teaching about the fundamental goodness of the creation: "God saw everything that he had made,
and indeed, it was very good" (Gen. 1:31).*

*The task of Christian theology is not to play these two
statements off against each other, but rather to find ways of
reconciling them. Rahner's strategy — one that by no means
all reputable theologians share — was to begin with the fundamental goodness of creation. For him, famously, original sin
was not a reality rampant in the cosmos until Jesus Christ came
along. Original sin was enfolded within a yet more original
grace — a grace that sin could not overpower. And grace, for
Rahner, means a sharing in God's very life: we too are divine
and human, temples of God's grace from the first moment of
our conception.*

*So in Rahner's theology, though Jesus certainly is "truly God
and truly human," this phrase cannot serve as a way of saying
why he is different from everyone else. Rahner has to account
for that rooted Christian conviction in another way. Rahner
presents Jesus, in particular his resurrection, as the once-for-
all and unrepeatable sign that the history of God's dealings
with the world has now entered on its final phase. To use his
technical language, Jesus is the Absolute Savior:*

> *We are applying this title to that historical person who
> appears in time and space and signifies the beginning
> of the absolute self-communication of God — a self-
> communication moving toward its end, that beginning
> which indicates that this self-communication for every-
> one has taken place irrevocably and has been victoriously
> inaugurated. . . . Savior here means that historical subjec-
> tivity in which, first, this process of God's absolute self-
> communication to the self-conscious world as a whole is*

present irrevocably; second, that event where this divine self-communication can be unambiguously recognized as irrevocable.... [2]

In the resurrection of Jesus, we have assurance. Though God's self-giving grace enfolds the whole of creation, and therefore the whole of our experience, we are ourselves consciously aware of it only in faith, amid darkness and ambiguity. The resurrection of Christ (and the assumption of Mary) serves to assure us that this otherwise uncertain history has begun to end, and that this end consists in God's triumph. That — no more but also no less — is the distinctive contribution of Christian witness.

It follows that what we say about Jesus — and about the tradition that stems from him in the saints, Scripture, tradition, and the Church — is always linked to a grace spread over the whole creation; no one is excluded from it. Jesus is not the exclusive locus of God's self-grace, but rather its inclusive focus. Faith in Jesus transforms us by freeing us from fear, by empowering us to live out fully human lives — and the mystery of God that suffuses them — without becoming anxious or embittered.

The first extract in this chapter comes again from Rahner's early book of prayers, Encounters with Silence. It asks the question why we can still pray, "Come, Lord Jesus" during Advent (its first publication was in the December issue of a devotional magazine), when Jesus has already come. Rahner's answer — already here anticipating his more theoretical statements much later — is that the truth of Jesus' first coming still needs to spread within the whole creation. God's self-gift, the universal bestowal of grace whereby God will be all in all, has been irrevocably begun: absolutely nothing can separate us from "the love of God in Christ Jesus our Lord" (Rom. 8:39). The second extract, from Mary, Mother of the Lord, a collection of Marian sermons given by Rahner in the 1950s, sketches out with

---

2. *Foundations of Christian Faith*, 195.

particular intensity and clarity how the truth of the Incarnation involves a rich account of God's presence within humanity at large.

GOD WHO IS MEANT TO BE COMING

Look, your Church's year has come to Advent again, my God. Again we are praying the prayers of longing and of waiting, the hymns of hope and promise. And over and over again all our needs and all our longing are gathering together into the one word, "Come." What a strange prayer. After all, you have already come and pitched your tent among us, you have shared our life with its small joys, its long daily drudge, and its bitter end. With our "come" can we be inviting you to anything more than that? *Could* you through your coming come any nearer to us than you did by entering so much into our normality that we can hardly now pick you out from other human beings, O God, you who have called yourself the Son of Man? And yet we pray: "come." And yet this word still comes from our hearts as it did from the patriarchs, kings, and prophets who saw your day only from far off and blessed it.

Is it just that *we are celebrating* Advent, or is it still *actually* Advent? Have you in fact really come — you in person, you whom we were thinking of when we yearned for the One who was to come, the mighty God, the Father of the world to come, the Prince of peace, the light, the truth, the happiness that is eternal? On the first pages of Holy Scripture your coming is already promised, and yet there still stands on its last page, to which not a single thing will now be added, the prayer "Come, Lord Jesus!"

Are you the eternal Advent, the one who always is to come and who never comes in such a way that all expectation becomes fulfillment? Are you the irretrievably distant one, toward whom all times and generations, all yearnings of hearts make pilgrimage, on roads that will never end? Are you just the distant horizon enfolding the land of our deeds and our suffering, always remaining equally distant, wherever we might wander? [...]

You were meant to come in order to redeem us from ourselves, and you — yes even you, the uniquely free and boundless One — have still "become," "become like us." And even if I know that you remain who you were, did you not recoil, you immortal One, at our mortality, you the expansive One at our narrowness, you the One of truth at our pretense? Have you not crucified yourself on to your own creation, by accepting for yourself as your own life, utterly intimately, utterly your own, what you had previously in your eternal distance just spread out as the dark, neutral background for your unapproachable light? Isn't the cross of Golgotha just the making visible of the cross that towers over the expanses of eternity, prepared by yourself for yourself?

Is this what your coming is? Have human beings made the immensity of history into one single great Advent choir — for even the one who curses you is still calling out within it — into one single call for you and your coming? Is it that our unhappiness is taken away from us because you too have wept? Is it that our self-surrender into our finitude is no longer the most terrible form of our desperation, because you too have said the words of surrender through your becoming human? Is it that our way, which recoils from its ending, has after all — just...us — a blessed ending?

But how can this be? Why can it be? How can our life — just because it's become yours — be the redemption from our life? How can you, having yourself come under the Law, thereby ransom us from the Law (Gal 4:5)? Just because my surrender into my life is an "Amen" to your human life, a "yes" to your coming that confounds all my expectations, does this make that surrender of mine the beginning of freedom from its burdensome constraint?

But how does it help *me* if my fate is now a participation in yours, and if you have just made what is mine yours? Or have you made my life just *the beginning* of *your* coming, the beginning of your life?

Slowly I am understanding once again what I have always known: you are still *in the process of coming,* and your appearance in the form of a servant is the *beginning* of your coming, which brings redemption from the servitude you took on. Ways that you travel along do have an end. Constraints that you take on do become free. The cross that you carry does become a sign of victory. It is not actually that you have come; you are still coming. From your becoming human till the fullness of this time is only the twinkle of an eye — and this is so even if millennia go by in its course, and thus, blessed by you, become a tiny part of this twinkle — the one twinkle of an eye that marks your one action, the action that gathers us all, and our whole destiny, into your human life and its fate, and brings us home into the eternal expanses that are the life of God.

Because you have begun on this ultimate action of yours in your creation, then ultimately nothing new can happen any more in this time, but rather, at the deepest level of reality, all times are now standing still: on us "the ends of the ages have come" (1 Cor. 10:11); only one single time remains in this world: your Advent. And when this last day comes to its end, there will be no more time, but just you in your eternity. [. . .]

It is deeds that determine what time is — it's not time that gives deeds and actions their permanence. A new action can inaugurate a new age. So with your Incarnation a new age has broken in, the final age. For what could now ever come to be that is not already borne within the womb of this age? Perhaps that we could come to be part of you? But that's just what has now happened, because you have deigned to become part of our human reality.

People say that you will come again. That is true. But it is not really "again," since you in your being human, a being that you have taken eternally to yourself as your own, have never left us. It is just that it must become more and more evident that you have come in reality, that the heart of all things is already now transformed because you have taken them to your heart. It is just that this coming must happen more and more, just that it must become more and more evident what has already begun in the ground of all that exists, just that your coming must dissolve into itself the mirage that suggests that finitude did not become free when you took it into your life. Behold, you are coming. This is neither past nor future, but present — a present that is just still filling itself out. It is still the one hour of your coming; and when this hour has come to an end, we will also know from experience that you have really come. Let me live in this hour of your coming so that I can live in you, O God who is to come! Amen.   — from *Encounters with Silence*, 79–87

MARY IN THEOLOGY

There is really a *human* theology, a proclamation of the faith and a theology that praise and glorify God by their saying something about humanity. Why is this?

First, God really is all in all. There is nothing alongside God that would of itself be worthy of mention when the faith is proclaimed and theology being done. In a real sense, one cannot in this holy house of God say anything, praise or mention anything except the eternal God, and God alone. Before God, everything else sinks into the abyss of its absolute insignificance. In theology and in faith it is not that there is God and then anything else you might think of; there is only the one God, past all grasp, thrice holy, worthy of adoration. When the heart reflects, makes confession, and raises itself to God, everything else must fall silent, everything else must be passed over in silence. Then the human person can do no greater deed than what we call the adoration, the blessing of this God. For after all, the life of faith and the effort of theology are meant to be growing into that one life whose entire content is the loving gaze on God face to face, the eternal praise of the grace that is God's alone.

And nevertheless, there is a theology of *humanity,* a Creed that says something about humanity itself, and this not alongside a profession of faith in the sole eternal God, but right within this profession itself. Why is this so? Because God, God's own self, God in God's tripersonal life, God in God's ineffable glory, God in God's eternal life, has taken us into this eternal life that is God's own. There is no need, as a poet of our day has said, for us to be dead so that God can be alive. God has not just given us something, something that God has created out of nothing; God has, beyond all that, given us God's own self. God has called us out of nothingness so that we can truly be; God has given us freedom so that we can really and truly be God's partners in God's presence. God has established a covenant with us. God's will was not just to deal with us through the creation, with what we encounter remaining just the finite and bearing within itself a sign or a mere pointer toward a God always still remaining beyond. God's will has been to deal with us as God's *self,* with what happens and what God does, what God shows and what God gives, ultimately nevertheless being really God's *self* — even if now only in the promise that God will one day show Godself to us face to face, with nothing remaining between God and us. Thus — this is the mystery of faith that is most worthy of adoration — God's own self in God's own Word has become *human.*

And if this is true, if it is part of the mystery of our God that this God is not just the God of the philosophers but the God of

Abraham, Isaac, and Jacob, and indeed, what is more, the Father of our Lord Jesus Christ, then for us Christians there is no profession of faith in the eternal God apart from our praising God as the one who has given His own self to us — and so much so that we can truly profess faith regarding one who is human that "he sits at the right hand of the eternal God" — so much so that we really and truly cannot do theology any more without also talking about humanity, doing anthropology — so much so that we can no longer say who God is in the truth and reality of the actual life God lives without saying that God's eternal word, in which God expresses God's very self, is humanity for all eternity.

Today, in a Christianity subsequent to Christ's birth, we cannot say anything true, authentic, and specific about God without professing faith in God as Emmanuel, as God-with-us, as the God of our flesh, as the God of our human nature, as the God of our human signs in the sacrament, as the God of our altars, as the God who has been born here from the Virgin Mary and so, as a human being among us, is a human being and God in one Person. Because this human being is the true, acting, and living God, then within the sphere of faith and theology about God the face of a human being shines out. And thus this genuine theology really is of necessity — not just as an afterthought, but from within its central living reality a theology glorifying the human person, and precisely as such it praises God alone. And this is ultimately why there can be a Mariology, a doctrine of the blessed Virgin, of the Mother of our Lord. This is why Mariology is not just a part of the private biography of Jesus of Nazareth, in the end of no significance for our salvation, but rather a statement of faith itself, about a reality of faith without which there would be no salvation.

Then there comes a second point. We human beings are important for each other. What we mean for each other is not just a matter of our life's daily routine. It is not just that if we are here we have to have parents; not just that we are always dependent — biologically, in the visible life of the civil community, in art and learning — on a great human collectivity. It is not just for these reasons and in these respects that we are important for each other. No, also as regards our salvation we remain dependent on other human beings. This is perfectly obvious, and yet still very difficult to grasp. One might think we are important only for life here and now, or for external things, or at most as regards the earthly life of the mind. One might think: when it comes to how God stands to me and I stand to God, when we are dealing with the final decision about my eternity, when we are dealing with how I will ultimately come through when I am left completely isolated before the face of God by the remorseless loneliness of my death, then for this question I am one who is completely on my own, left to myself. Then there will remain only God-alone and me: God's heart, God's mercy, and my individual freedom of a guilt and a grace that are unavoidably my own.

And yet it is not like this. Everything said above is true, but it is not the whole truth. The whole truth is this: even then we are still part of each other. All persons have their own, inalienable, once-and-for-all freedom, from which they cannot run away, and which they cannot unload onto anyone else. But yet this does not mean that this freedom is an isolated freedom, not even when it is deciding the eternal fate of a human being, or when it is finally shaping a person's being forever. For the eternal Son, the eternal Word of the Father, has become flesh from the Virgin Mary. In our family, from our race that lives here between Adam the first human being and the last one, the Father's word has become flesh.

In nature and in grace, therefore, existence is a reality in common. This works itself out in a shared reality of sin and guilt, a shared reality of God's mercy and God's grace, a shared reality of origin and goal. But guilt and grace, beginnings and ends, are matters for God. And therefore this human reality in common extends into the sphere of human salvation before God. Human beings are in a communion of salvation and its opposite — a great communion that plays out, as a whole and not just in individual people, the great drama of history before God's face. And in this drama, it becomes clear what God has really thought about humanity. It is only these thousands, innumerable thousands of variations of humanity, in their harmonies and in their contradictions, that go to make up the one history of the world and together bring about what was really meant when God spoke in the beginning: "Let us make humanity in our own image and likeness."

— *Mary, Mother of the Lord*, 24–28

Another prayer from Encounters with Silence *brings out a corollary of Rahner's vision of Christ. Life can often be frustrating: what Rahner says here about his experience as a priest doing pastoral care applies far more widely. Yet we have assurance that precisely through these frustrating human interactions, God has chosen to work. We may not see how this is the case and simply have to hang on in faith, but that God works in and through our messy human dealings is certain. One acid test of devotion to Christ is our attitude to the unpromising human beings with whom he is one flesh.*

GOD OF MY SISTERS AND BROTHERS

O God, these people to whom you've thrown me out from my home with you! Mostly they won't accept me, your messenger, at all; they want nothing to do with your gifts, your grace, and your truth, with which you have sent me to them. And yet I must, like a pestering peddler, keep on even knocking at their doors. If I only knew that when they did not accept me, they really wanted to turn *you* away, that would give me consolation. But perhaps I too would quietly and without questioning keep the doors into the house that is my life closed if someone knocked in the way I do, with the claim of having been sent by you.

And as for those who do let me into the houses that are their lives! They normally want anything but what I am meant to be bringing from you. They want to tell me about their wretched, tiny concerns; they want to pour out their hearts to me. My God, what a conglomeration comes spilling out! What a horrendous mish-mash of the tragic and the comical, of small truth and big lies, of little pains that are taken too seriously and big sins that are made light of! And what do these people want of me? If it is not simply money, material help, or a little comfort from a sympathetic heart that they're seeking, they mostly look on me as some kind of insurance agent, with whom they can take out a heavenly accident policy to prevent your breaking in upon their lives in the omnipotence of your holiness and justice, shaking them out of their tiny everyday concerns and their narrow Sunday self-satisfaction. They just want to be left in peace for this life and for the next. How rarely does anyone say, "Lord, what are you wanting me to do?" How rarely does anyone really want to hear in its entirety and without strings the astounding message that we must love you passionately — love *you,* not just ourselves, you for your own sake, not just for our sake; and *love* you, not just respect you and worry about your judgment. How rarely does anyone want to confront the gift of your grace as it really is: tough, clear, not just for our consolation but also your glory, pure and upright, silent and bold. [. . .]

But look, my God — if with your grace and your truth — I go to people on something like an inspection trip, and knock on the door of their inner self, and if they let me in, they usually lead me only into the rooms in which they live their ordinary

daily lives. They tell me about themselves and their worldly affairs; they show me their poor earthly furniture. They talk a lot
about trivialities in order to stay away from the one real thing.
They try to make themselves and me forget why I have actually come, to bring you, my God, like the blessed sacrament
into that inmost chamber of their hearts where what is eternal
in them is sick unto death, where there ought to be an altar
prepared for you, on which the lights of faith, hope, and love
burn. Instead, they receive me into their everyday rooms. Into
these I can find a door easily. But in vain do I seek for a door
into where a person's eternal destiny is decided, into the ultimate depths of a person. It almost seems to me that there are
people who live their own lives so superficially that they themselves have never yet found the way and the doors to that place
where every human being is sick, whether unto death or life.

How am I meant to find the way there? Or is it that there
just isn't this kind of way for me? Am I the sort of messenger who just hands over your message and gift at the "delivery
entrance," without ever being allowed to enter into the "interior castle" of another's soul so as to be able to make sure that
your message and your gift really becomes eternal life for this
person through this person's free love. When this unique, decisive act of a human being happens, is it your will to be and
to act with that person quite alone in an innermost recess of
the heart? Is my "care of souls" at an end when I have done
"my duty" and carried out my orders? Is it that I neither can
nor should bring you into the ultimate depth of another person,
given that you are, after all, always there already: you who fill
all things, in whom each person lives and has being, you who
are always there already for the salvation or judgment of each
human person.

But if you have ordered me actually to care for souls and not
just to bother about "my duty," then this care of mine must
be able to get into that most hidden chamber of the other self,

into the innermost center, into their "spark of the soul." And if you alone have really found the way there, you in your grace, against whose gentle omnipotence no heart succeeds in sealing itself off when it wills to have mercy on a person, then I can know that you alone are the way I must go and the door through which I must pass in order to find the soul of my sister and brother. I must find my way to you, ever more deeply into you, if I am not to be just a more or less happily received and tolerated guest in the everyday life of the other person, if I am to be allowed to enter there where your eternal light or where eternal darkness dwells in humanity. For you are still within the most inward isolation of persons, their closed-in-on-themselvesness. You are sustaining them in your unsearchable love and omnipotence, to which even the kingdom which is the freedom of each individual person is still subject. Therefore, only the person who is there with *you* is there as a carer for souls, you, King of all hearts.

So then, you did not, after all, send me away from yourself when you gave me the task of going to people. Rather, through this kind of charge, you have just given me in a new way what is your only commandment: to find my way home to you in love. All care of souls — in its ultimate, true reality — is possible only in you, in your love that binds me to you and thus takes me with it also to the place to which you alone can still find a way: to human hearts. I find you in love, and in what — for true love of you — is life: in prayer. If I had prayed more, I would be closer to souls. For the prayer that does not just pester you for your gifts, but loves myself into you, is not just something that helps the care of souls along, but rather the first and last real act of that care.

Lord, teach me to pray, teach me to love you. Then I shall forget my own wretchedness, because then I will be able to do what wretchedness makes me forget to do: to bring the poverty of my sisters and brothers into your richness. In you, God of

my sisters and brothers, I will be able really to be a brother
to others, one who can help them in the one thing necessary:
finding you.   — from *Encounters with Silence*, 61–68

*The next extract comes from a retreat conference that Rahner
gave to seminarians in the 1950s and spells out how faith in
Christ should, in his view, shape our decisions.*[3] *It is not simply
a question of following the commandments or the dictates of
right reason. We have, rather, to discern the particular quality
of our discipleship with Christ and be prepared to make decisions that are right for us, even when they would be wrong for
others.*

ON THE FOLLOWING OF CHRIST

What It Is to Follow Christ

I have already suggested that the most central feature in the
world's constitution is that it forms the "surroundings," the
"life-space" for the God who, in person, "becomes world" —
so much so that the fact that the world could exist at all is
grounded in the fact that the Incarnation could happen (a point
that would still be valid even if this fundamental divine possibility had not come about). There is therefore no human person
whose reason for being here is in the end anything other than
to make this adventure of love for what lies outside Himself
possible for God — and to make this possible through a life
and existence shared with the Word made human. For this purpose, God really does need humanity, because the finite human
person, such as God became, is essentially oriented to his or

---

3. The text was taken down by the seminarians as Rahner delivered it. Perhaps
significantly, there is no Rahnerian manuscript of this chapter underlying the printed
text.

her other, his or her human companions. Therefore, the whole human race is in this sense centered, from the beginning, on the Son of Man as the core of its meaning. From the beginning, the human race is the "filling out [*pleroma*] of Christ."

But if the concrete life of Jesus of Nazareth (and the whole point of our lives for each one of us is to share in living that life) is not something added on to the Incarnation but *itself* the appearance, the enactment, the presence of God's own Word, of God's own life; if in this concrete life of Jesus God's innerness is opened to us without reserve and in a way that cannot be surpassed; if God's innerness has here come upon us — then to become part of this life, to let oneself go into it, is already to become part of the inner-divine life, already the entry into a burning eternity such that it is an eternal mystery why we do not disintegrate when it comes before us. If all this is so, then to look at the countenance of the human being, Jesus of Nazareth, is already to experience the vision of God face to face, despite the obvious fact that both of these, the encounter with Jesus and the vision of God's self that occurs in this encounter, come to their decisive breakthrough only when the deceptive narrowness of our former flesh is broken apart in death. Jesus said: "Have I been with you all this time, Philip, and you still do not know me? Whoever has seen me has seen the Father. How can you say, 'Show us the Father?' " (John 14:9).

So grace, the drawing of our being into the innerness of the divine life, is not an abstract, arbitrary divinization, to be understood in purely metaphysical terms, as if, though "merited" by Christ, it were fundamentally independent of him. It is not as though grace were brought about by a loving will of God that was in itself transhistorical, equally coexistent with every moment of human history, a love *always* coming into the world at any old time or place. Rather, grace is a concrete assimilation to Christ, a becoming part of *his* life. Thus it is the grace *of Christ,* not just in the sense that Christ has merited it for us, but in the full ontological[4] sense.

We must not water this participation in Jesus' life down to a matter merely of ethics, so to speak, or of the imagination. Any moral influence that Jesus has must be dependent, fundamentally, on a very real, ontological influence. As a result of our essential orientation to the Incarnation of the Word, we are drawn into the life of Jesus by the very fact of this Incarnation, and by the whole history of his living and dying. The whole world, and in particular the life of each one of us, is really affected, specified, and fundamentally shaped by Jesus' existence.

In narrower, historically accessible terms, we were then through baptism made members of the community that is his body, and thus drawn even deeper into his life through this sacramental mark on the historical reality of our lives. Something similar can be said of all the sacraments: they are at once a sign and a strengthening of the attraction toward the life of Jesus, toward the beating with the rhythm of his existence that has unwaveringly taken hold of the whole creation (given that its most central characteristic is its being the surroundings for Christ) — even though this most intimate and rich reality of our lives will become clear (which is not the same as "effective" or "making a difference") only when the shadows of this life fall away.

And if even to ourselves our rhetoric on this matter seems so remote from how we sense things directly, so pale and abstract, nevertheless it is valid: in our being taken up in this way into the

---

4. This barbarism of technical theology (most of the time when people use this pretentious word they would do better to say "real") is important here. Rahner, following Heidegger, uses this term to refer to the reality of personal relations, whereas for most Catholic theologians "ontological" — used to denote the change that comes with ordination, for example — means something like a mere change in substance. (Rahner's sniffy jargon for this usage is "ontic.")

concrete, historical, life of Jesus of Nazareth — a concrete historical reality that is thus a presence for us — our entry into the
blessedness of the triune, inner-divine life is already happening.

So far we have thought of our taking part in Jesus' life more
in terms of its being a reality prior to any free attitude of ours,
more in terms of its specifying our "nature" (as opposed to our
"person").[5] But this life of our Lord that is already, always and
necessarily, working on us "calls" to our freedom, so that our
freedom too, of itself, can affirm that life, entrust itself to it
and become part of it, and so that as a result the grace that is
revealed in him might truly then come to be ours.

We can shut ourselves off from this call. We can stop the law
of Jesus' life from also being the law of our lives. We can try as
it were to eliminate Jesus' life from our lives, so far as within
us lies. But ultimately we will never succeed. Even if we reject it
personally, it remains the most central constituent of humanity.
The only thing that will be achieved through such attempts will
be — literally — that they change heaven into hell.

But if we listen to this "call" and let ourselves go into the life
of Jesus working on us in faith and love, then fundamentally
what we call "the following of Christ" is already happening in
us. Obviously this following [...] can take place on very different levels of reflective awareness, depending on whether the
figure of Jesus is present in a person's life only anonymously, as
it were, or whether, beyond this, Jesus' self-revelation in word
and deed, the gospel as Scripture and as preaching, has reached
that person. It will depend too on how far the person interprets
correctly or falsely how this following should be carried out and
on the correct or false links that the person makes between such
a judgment and their "historical knowledge" of the life of Jesus.

---

5. Again, Rahner uses these terms rather differently from other theologians of
his time. "Person" refers to those elements in our lives that are subject to our
freedom; "nature" to the givens that are not.

Even if we believe that genuine following of Christ is possible where the "historical knowledge" of Jesus' life, mediated through Scripture and the Church, has not yet arrived, this is in no way to undervalue the gospel's significance. The Word of God willed to reveal himself in such a way that he enters the world as a visible, public epiphany of grace and remains in the world until its end — not as a historical force working anonymously. It follows that a life following the Word revealed in this way must be publicly warranted in the same way as the Word is; it must relate expressly (helped by Scripture and tradition) to the "historical" Jesus; it must understand itself as part of his *pleroma;*[6] in a word, it must be "ecclesiastical."

This need, however, is not simply to be derived from a formulated divine command. It is also more than a mere requirement to pay due respect (on the ground that it befits the "dignity" of the Incarnate Son of God that even in this earthly life he is not just the secret center of the creation, recognized by a few at most, but already now publicly honored and loved as the King of the Universe). Rather, it is only a permanent reference to the "historical" Jesus, only constantly repeated contemplation of the mysteries of his life, only the listening again and again to his words that enable any following of Jesus to attain self-understanding and thus to grow to fullness. Only if we look at Jesus of Nazareth and listen to his word that comes to us "from outside" will it become clear to us what we are, and always have been: those whose basis and reason for living is the incarnate, eternal Word who in Jesus of Nazareth is publicly present to the world.

In other respects our following of the Lord must remain obscure: the free "yes" of our freedom that it involves is possible only indirectly and implicitly; it stands in permanent danger of being misunderstood and of really becoming lost in this

---

6. The Pauline term meaning "fullness."

misunderstanding, because our reflective awareness is not just "reflective," secondary, but rather has a feedback effect, thus helping shape and direct what occurs in the depths of the soul. Therefore we must try to make our following of Jesus a conscious reality; we must exercise it and cultivate it; as we grow in this Christ-life that has been already given to us, we must, of our own accord so to speak, hold up the form and structure for such life that we can see in unambiguous clarity only in the "historical" Jesus. (It is for this reason, let me say in passing, that Ignatius requires meditation on the mysteries of Jesus' life.)

Our task is to get some theological purchase on the idea of the following of Christ. Only that will enable us to understand the Second Week of the Exercises properly. In the meditations that follow, we should always keep before our eyes these two things that have emerged from the reflections just offered:

1. The following of Christ is not the observance of moral rules that, although perhaps exemplified by Jesus, fundamentally derive their validity and can be known independently of him. Rather it is an actively participative resonance with precisely his life, and in that life with the inner-divine life that has been given to us.

2. The call to follow Christ is not just a matter of words that come from outside only to direct us along a path alien to our nature. Rather, and ultimately, it is the necessary unfolding of what we are in ourselves and always have been: those who are destined in the deepest part of our being for life with Christ.

Following Christ: Its Formal Structure

On the basis of what has just been sketched out about what it is to follow Christ, the first thing to be said is that it must involve a decision on the part of each person regarding that person's own individual style of following.

In the Incarnation the Word emptied himself into his human nature, a nature that is essentially orientated toward a human other. If human persons are to find their own existence, they need those who are human with them genuinely to be other, to be different, i.e., precisely not clones. Human beings find their own perfection only in the otherness of those who are human with them, an otherness acknowledged, affirmed, and sheerly loved. This applies also to Christ, indeed especially so. We must say also of him: insofar as the Word made human loves human beings as others and because they are others, he too attains the fullness of his nature. He becomes what he is meant to be in his humanity, in a true historical presence, only — really only — through his being our brother and affirming our validity as others. This point was not always as clear as in itself it should have been. There have certainly been attempts in the history of the Church to copy the life of Jesus as precisely as possible, as for example in the controversy about Franciscan poverty.

Thus, the genuine following of Christ in a communion of life with him consists in letting the inner law of his life work itself out in situations that will always be new, always different, depending on the person involved. It is only when we thus continue his life in an active way and do not try simply to repeat it over and over again (*that* will be like using a photocopier with the toner running out) that the following of Jesus is something worth living out, only then that it is of any interest to God's own self, and only then that it can mean we attain eternity with the Son of Man raised to God's right hand. And what makes it truly and genuinely the following of Jesus is that it maintains the inner law of that life by virtue of its taking place in the power of his Spirit, God's Holy Spirit poured out upon us.

Because this continuing of Christ's life occurs in situations that are always new and always specifically mine, the concrete form in which it applies for me is something I always need to be finding in new ways. A specific historical situation is more than the product of general laws of history. Equally, my way of following Christ cannot simply be deduced from the general laws governing such following — although these laws do exist. Such discovery is always an individual, inalienable decision. Thus an essential aspect of the following of Christ is the taking of responsibility for what no one, no ethics text book and no spiritual director, can tell us. But therefore we must also take upon ourselves the risk of the loneliness involved in such existential decision-making. We must not try to load this responsibility onto some outside agent — a tendency that often underlies people's hunt for the ideal confessor.

Obviously this is not a charter for indulging a narcissistic introversion that has no desire other than that of self-development. Since one cannot save even one's soul except by losing it, human persons bring their existence to maturity by developing it in service, in selfless sacrifice, and in the spending of oneself for others.

A second consequence of what I have been saying about what it is to follow Christ is that following Christ is fundamentally an act of obedience, however much it also involves the making of one's own decisions and the assuming of responsibility for oneself.

However much the following of Our Lord must always be my following, it must also exhibit quite specific features that mark it out as the following of Christ rather than of anyone else. It must have some basic structures that anyone who wants to enter into Christ's life must hold to, and indeed accept in obedience — *prior* to the necessarily individual way in which such a person's following is shaped. However, Christ's once-and-for-all life and act is a manifestation of God's sovereign grace that cannot be evaluated by any other standard, and thus its demands cannot be derived, in the way the natural law is, from general facts about our existence. Nevertheless, this concrete historical event does imply a law that binds all people, the "new Law" that he has given us in word and deed and that we have to read off from the story of his life.

Moreover, the inalienable decision through which each of us has to find the concrete form for our following is also itself an act of obedience: the hearing of the individual imperative from God, God who has placed me into my situation in order that I might carry forward Christ's life in a way befitting this situation; the submissive love that has no desire to make independent and self-centered projections for even the most personal flourishing of what is its own, but rather still to be receiving even this from the hand of God. More precisely, fealty toward Christ, who faces me concretely, one person to another, and who, in his freedom against which no appeal is possible, allocates me my place in his retinue of disciples.

In the following of Christ, then, decisions for oneself and subordination to Christ are not in contradiction with each other: both are essential, fundamentally inseparable aspects of the one act of surrender to the Lord. But their relationship is nevertheless one in which opposites must be held together. You will not always find harmony between them easy to achieve or painless. The tension between them is something quite characteristic of Christian existence. However this tension works out, Christ wants us to follow him in radical obedience; he does not, however, want us just to trot along after him (which would be much easier). Each one of us has a task to fulfill in Christ's name, and no one can take this task away from us. Obedience to the universally applicable law of Christ and courage to find one's personal way (which is in fact nothing but the most radical form of obedience) — both follow equally from what it is to be a disciple of the Lord. That both of these are involved is at once the difficulty and the greatness of our existence as Christians.   —*Spiritual Exercises*, 114–21

The final long extract in this chapter comes from a talk that Rahner gave in the Innsbruck seminary in 1966. It argues that devotion to the Sacred Heart, which Rahner would have known in a mass-sentimental form that he could see was dying, nevertheless is an attempt to represent something of perennial importance and of special relevance in the post-Christian age in which we find ourselves now. There is a clericalism in the writing that cannot be fully edited out — but this piece represents in a particularly striking way Rahner's ability to answer questions about the Church's future, not by abandoning or transforming the tradition, but by mining it for new significance. Once again, too, it brings out how Rahner's devotion to Jesus goes together with his openness to everyday experience, however painful or ambiguous.

THE MAN WITH THE PIERCED HEART

It would be stupid and cowardly to want to avoid recognizing that the history of devotion to the heart of Jesus has entered a critical phase. Will it, effectively, die out in the Church? Die not so much from the loud protests of those who reject it, but rather from the taken-for-granted silence, the simple lapsing of those who no longer relate to it, cannot relate to it? (At most they are aware of it as a historical relic that you find here and there, like a chapel of the Fourteen Holy Helpers, or like an Infant Jesus of Prague that in the old days used to decorate Great-Grandmother's chest of drawers and is still hanging around in a Christian family.) In twenty years time, will there be anything more left to Sacred Heart devotion than an official, liturgical feast, one like many others that began as liturgical expressions of a living piety and that then did not disappear, given the conservative tendencies of the liturgy, even though the life that brought them about has long been extinguished.

In twenty years time, will there still be First Fridays in the parishes? Or will it just be a few pious people, perhaps in convents, who "keep the Nine First Fridays," as we say — mere relics of what the sociology of religion sees as a previous age that is now basically past? In twenty years time (time goes fast these days) will people hear the phrase, "Heart of Christ" — wherever it still turns up — with surprise, like a word from a linguistic register that is no longer their own? Will people therefore have first to make a great effort to explain what the phrase actually means, and why people use this particular expression to talk about the reality to which it refers.

Now you can certainly hold that *some part* of these symptoms of crisis can be traced back to particular circumstances that should not remain, circumstances that, given the abiding presence of the Spirit to the Church, we can simply say *will* not remain: a certain hectic drivenness among Christians and the clergy; a certain rationalistic barrenness of the heart; a vanishing of the contemplative and the mystical in the Church; the lack of a prayerful theology; the temptation to expect everything wholesome in the Church to come from institutional changes alone. But even taking all that into account, and even if you expect that a new spring of the contemplative and the mystical will follow on from this present winter, and in a new form, this is still not enough to answer fully the question raised by the crisis situation of Sacred Heart devotion.

In the Church, history does not just "happen." It comes about through decisions made by hearts of faith, hearts open to grace. The real question to ask is, therefore, not "What is going to happen?" but rather "What is the future that I am going to opt for, under the vocation and the grace that is at once my burden and my identity?" And you ask this question so that you can do what you are meant to do, and leave everything else to the silent sovereignty of the Lord of history. After all, it is quite clear: those who in the end just pore over the question of how successful their decision, their action in history, is going to be, those who are seeking from the outset to align themselves with what seem the big battalions, those who do not have the courage to stay loyal to what is contradicted and seems to have no chance — in the end these people are cowards, and fundamentally lack any real conscience. They are objects, not subjects, of history. And this applies in the Church of the crucified one as well: victory is for those whose position is hopeless, who hope against all hope.

Given this, I have the courage to say that it can be an unspeakably holy grace, even for the priest of tomorrow, to understand what "Sacred Heart" and "Sacred Heart devotion" mean. I would like to try to explain this thesis a little.

In the thesis as I have put it, I have already implicitly qualified what I am saying in two ways. First, I am not talking about the popular piety of tomorrow. This is not because I wanted to prophesy that Sacred Heart devotion would in effect disappear from such piety — who can say that? Nevertheless, it is imaginable that God might will and even judge that the average Christian (and there will still be average Christians tomorrow) will not arrive explicitly at this mystery — to talk expressly in these terms to such people would be too much. It might therefore be that this devotion — as it was in the Middle Ages — will become more esoteric in character. But even if one accepted that much, this is still far short of saying that such devotion could not be a grace for a small circle, for a holy remnant of those whom it catches hold of, for the witnesses, for the spirituality that can be a fruitful and authentic model for others, for a circle to which priests too should belong.

Second: my thesis says "can." It is therefore not saying that all versions of priestly spirituality that are genuine and authentic must always necessarily recognize themselves expressly and by name in anything calling itself "Sacred Heart devotion." All

I am saying is that this *could* happen. And such a possibility, which is on offer in the Church's approved practice for today and tomorrow too, should not be rejected by persons — in the particular form they find it — before humble, mature testing has revealed it to be something that nevertheless is not really for them.

Now, this is quite possible. And why not? In the Father's house there are many mansions. If individual Christians' piety, their spirituality, tries to bring forth on the one tree that is their own life all the fruits that have ever grown in the garden of the Church, this is not a genuine spirituality for a human being who is, in all humility, finite, and simply one member of the Church that is always more than an individual can be. And this does not apply just to St. Anthony devotion. It applies too to explicit, more or less significant and intense, Sacred Heart devotion — though it certainly applies here more than to such things as devotion to Our Lady. But to recognize this realistically does not prevent us from saying that Sacred Heart devotion can be a great grace for priestly life, a grace that is not — once it has been offered — to be haughtily despised or lightly written off as personally unreal.

To explain my claim, I would like to start with a question. What will tomorrow's priests have to be, what will they look like, if they are to be more or less up to their vocation? I don't think I have to be a prophet to be able to answer this by saying that they will need to be — more so even than is already the case today — something more than mere functionaries of an institutional style of religion that carries itself forward by its own power in society. It will not be so much that the Church authenticates them as that they authenticate the Church. They will not be able to use their office as a form of social prestige; instead they will have to guarantee and bear witness to its validity through the manifestation of the Spirit and of power, through an experience of God that is authentic and living. They won't be able to operate as officials, exercising a religious and social function as if it were a bourgeois job with precisely defined duties, and then be able — finally — to be private citizens, whose lives no one interferes with. They must be people of faith, hope, and love, and these as matters of completely authentic experience. In the end their job cannot be learned. Indeed, if you look fully at all the implications it demands, it is not simply something that is transmitted through the sacramental laying on of hands, *ex opere operato*. It is a charism — even more so than that of a sage or a poet — a charism that has to be lived out in the social body that is the Church, and also (for all that the way this happens is now changing) in secular society. Their lives must be invested in their vocations; their vocations must still remain their lives even when they cannot be exercised any longer as a job in the conventional sense. It is like how we can distinguish real musicians from those who just do it as a job: some are musicians because music feeds them; others remain musicians even though this means that they starve.

Tomorrow's priest will be a person to whom mature people find their way, even though civil society is no longer driving its children in that direction. They will be people who truly share the heavy darkness of human life with all their brothers and sisters, knowing that this darkness has at once its first origin and its blessed fulfillment in that love that conquers through the past-all-graspness of the cross. Tomorrow's priest will be a person who can listen (otherwise there won't be any priests), a person to whom every individual is important, even when they mean nothing politically or socially. They will be people to whom others can entrust themselves, people who practice, try to practice, the holy folly of carrying not only their own burden, but also the burden of others. They will have what it takes, and will not be weaklings — but they will not collude in the hopeless, neurotic quest for money, pleasure, and other things that we use as painkillers in face of life's horrendous disappointments. Instead they will show in their lives that free renunciation is a possibility in the love of the crucified one, and that this renunciation is liberating. Tomorrow's priests will not be those who derive their power from a socially powerful Church, but who rather have the courage to let the Church make them powerless. They will believe that life comes from death, and that there is enough of God's power in love, in selflessness, in the Word of the cross, and in grace to bring about what in the end is the only thing that matters: namely, that individuals hand themselves over to the past-all-graspness of their lives willingly, in faith and hope that here God's past-all-graspness is in control as salvation and as the forgiving love that imparts itself.

Tomorrow's priests will be the people who are least able to justify themselves in secular terms, because their real success will always be disappearing into the mystery of God: they are precisely not psychotherapists going round in old-fashioned uniforms looking like the Magi. They will speak gently; they will not think they can pompously, by argument, argue life's darkness and the constant struggle for faith into the light. Calmly they will let God conquer where they are defeated. They will still see God's grace at work where they themselves can no longer bring it with word and sacrament in such a way that precisely in the bringing it is accepted. They will not measure the power of grace in terms of membership statistics, and yet they will know that they themselves are a very part of God's own service and mission, even if they are also convinced that God's mercy can do its work without them.

In a word: tomorrow's priests will be people with pierced hearts, from which alone the power of their mission will come. Pierced hearts: pierced by life's godlessness, pierced by love's folly, pierced by failure, pierced by the sense of their own wretchedness and their own deep ambiguity. But also people of faith that only through such a heart can the power of their mission be communicated. The authority that comes from office, the objective validity of the Word, the *ex opere operato* effectiveness of the sacraments — all these are transformed into an event of salvation by God's grace only when they come to human beings through this ineffable core that is a pierced heart. I say that tomorrow's priests are people with pierced hearts because it is their role to lead people to the innermost center of their beings, to the ground of their own hearts. And they can do this only if they have found their own heart — and this center of being, this heart, can be found by themselves and by others only if its piercedness is accepted, the piercedness from love's past-all-graspness that has willed to be victorious only in death.

Of course you can say, rightly, that priests have always had to be like this, that they must always be like this. But just this, which has, as people say, always been a part of priestly life, is being demanded now and in the future more overtly and more inevitably as a matter of the priest's own decision. For priesthood is becoming less and less a reality taken for granted in society. More and more it must be lived out in a diaspora amid a lack of faith, in a Church that means not very much in society, in a world where people cannot begin with God. Indeed one has to ask whether the priest's social status as it now still is will not be reduced a great deal further in the future (which is certainly not to say that the form we can imagine this status taking will be what we already now are having to strive for and promote).

But in any case, the Constantinian period is coming to an end, not only for the Church in general, but for each individual priest. No longer can priests handle their mission from within a little state-like Church; no longer do they function in villages like little popes; no longer do they count without question among the notables; their social privileges and prestige are vanishing. Gradually they are coming to have only what they should actually *be:* an identity as a person of God, a *homo religiosus,* a person living in faith, hoping, loving. They are being asked by the situation in which they live whether they really are what who are meant to be: people with pierced hearts that are true temples of God, sources of the Spirit, and the real power of their vocation and credibility.

Tomorrow's priests, who have to be like this, may well always feel overwhelmed by what they should be, and indeed — in an ultimate depth through God's grace — actually are. They will be full of concern and ask where they are meant to find what they do not themselves have — even though they can always see with utter simplicity and clarity what they are meant to be. Then there is only one thing they can do: turn to their Lord whom they are serving, look on the one whom they have pierced, and honor the pierced heart of Jesus Christ.

Once again (before I try to say what I have just said again, more clearly), remember the two qualifications I have already mentioned. Remember too everything we know about how "heart" is a central concept in the Bible; that the word is a primary word, referring to individuals' authentic center, where they stand as one flesh-and-blood reality before God; that "heart" is not something said metaphorically, as a result of some artificial transfer of meaning from the physiological organ. "Heart" fundamentally means the person's center, where a person's eternity dwells, where it comes to be. Human beings need such basic words that conjure up archetypes of this kind. Otherwise they will wither in a rationalistic desert and in effect know nothing about the mystery of their being except what they can find words for — and that means that ultimately they will not know anything at all, because their words will have lost the reference to what transcends them, to a more primordial experience in which the human person's own self, God and God's Spirit, are present, precisely in the heart. Remember too that Sacred Heart devotion involves naming the Lord's heart, but not, essentially, that the Lord's heart itself becomes a direct object of prayer and of cultic invocation — it is quite enough, and indeed (where too much feeling would be inappropriate) better, to call on the Lord himself "in his heart," to seek him and love him "looking on his heart."

So, bearing in mind our two qualifications and what has just been said, we can declare: "tomorrow's priests will find their own truth and reality when they look on the Lord's heart." Here is the heart that has admitted the world's darkness, its sin, into itself; the heart that gathered even its own Godforsakenness into the hands of the Father; the heart that wanted no power except that of forgiving love; the heart that was pierced and so became the source of everything that is of the Spirit. Here is the heart of the world, the core in which God and world, eternity and time, life and death, God's word and humanity's answer became one, without separation or confusion. Here the unity of substance that we call the hypostatic union is translated into something that happens in real life, and only thereby attains what this phrase actually means, only thereby finally comes to what it should be.

Here everything that the Father's Word Made Flesh brings about, and therefore the many different kinds of experience we have of Him, is united and reconciled in its origin. When we say, "Sacred Heart," then we are evoking the primordial, unifying center, past-all-grasp and therefore at the same time to be understood in its own terms — the center that unfolds itself and brings itself to completion in the story of Jesus of Nazareth, the center that alone gives meaning both to this story and, within it, to every event whatever: the meaning that is of God, of God's past-all-graspness, of God's love, of the life that finds itself in death.

This heart is not "sweet" but terrifying. Terrifying in its dark death-agony; terrifying in the past-all-grasp mystery of Love in which God sets God's own self at the mercy of God's creation, with its guilt and futility. Terrifying in the absoluteness of this heart's challenge, drawing us into its fate. Terrifying in the trust that it brings to our appalling ambiguity. If we do say that this heart is "sweet," then this refers to the holy maturity of the love that conquers in death, a maturity understood only by those who have accompanied such love as it has suffered its terrifying fate.

This pierced heart is what tomorrow's priests must encounter. Do not think that this Sacred Heart devotion is old-fashioned, something belonging to a style of spirituality that has now passed. What is old-fashioned? What is contemporary? The really contemporary Christian is not the person who observes a fleeting nonconformity regarding the past, falls victim to the present, and mistakes what is merely flashy and surface-deep for what is of the future. The contemporary Christian is rather the person who preserves what is ancient and anticipates the true future.

In the Church, what often is only apparently old is where, frequently, the future is being anticipated before it has arrived in a way that all and sundry can see. At a time of naive individualism, some people had the courage to follow a truly ecclesial spirituality. These people were already anticipating the period that is now just beginning. Those who followed Ignatius and really made the Exercises with a view to making a fundamental choice in their lives were already anticipating a genuine theological existentialism of solitary decision — something that perhaps will not really arrive until tomorrow. But it is these rare people, the people who decide for themselves and find what belongs to tomorrow in what was of yesterday — these are the people who really sustain what is truly of today.

And it can also be like this with Sacred Heart devotion. Ultimately it has little to do with the Baroque. It is not about superfluous religious introversion, the cult of a beautiful soul — it is not a luxury that has become foreign to our scanty, radically threatened age. For here we are adoring the heart that has forgotten itself into the deathly loneliness of our guilt, into the fearful past-all-graspness of God, and therefore also into the laborious service of daily fidelity. The Baroque stem was only there to enable the growth of the grain of wheat that today is dying and falling into the earth, and that tomorrow will bring forth fruit: the fruit that is the power for decision of the solitary heart; the fruit that is faith amid unbelief; the fruit that is an experience of God within a world that is crying out, whether casually or anxiously, "God is dead"; the fruit that is mutual love (and this love is something other than the cunning and violent calculations of everyone's mutual egoism); the fruit that is the folly of the cross and the courage to die in a world that believes it has overcome death because it hides the dying in hospitals and thinks it is bringing about life when it is just prolonging the death-agony.

The human heart is always an unknown land that only the future will discover, a first beginning where we are always in a state of not having yet arrived. And therefore the understanding of the Sacred Heart in faith, hope, and love is the one long and always new adventure that comes to an end only when we have arrived at our own heart and discovered that this dreadful pit is nevertheless filled by God. This applies to individuals, and it also applies to our shared situation in the present.

Abstract reflections like these about the history of ideas and the history of theology are never going to lecture anyone into a decision to adore the Sacred Heart; still less are the artifices of theology going to engender the grace and the charism that such devotion is. These enable us to do only one thing: to draw attention to the question that each of us must answer for ourselves: "Does what these words refer to meet up with what comes from the most intimate center of our being in the way we are talking about?" These words are understood only if grace itself empowers the human person's ground with what these words proclaim. But if persons have the courage to experience

God, in other words the courage for the heart's loneliness, the courage for fidelity and the unrewarded conscience, the courage to love the most remote persons as if they were a neighbor, then they discover their own wretched heart and begin to understand what "heart" actually means.

And if these persons, in faith and in prayer, in hope and in love, turn to their Lord, the Son of Man, in order to find in Him the image in which they themselves are created and toward which they are called, then, suddenly and with a blessed shock, they will see how, out of the experience of their own hearts, they are calling on this Lord of theirs through his own heart.

They will notice that the grace of Sacred Heart devotion is being offered to them. They will accept it; they will make efforts to let it grow — discreetly, without any to-do of high-flown pious rhetoric, and without ignoring the inevitable pluralism among creatures even when it comes to religion, a religion that has to be expressed in all kinds of different ways in order to do the one thing that everything turns on. They will notice that the silent austerity characteristic of today's spirituality is not to be lamented: it is simply forming the sphere of solitude and silence recommended to us, the sphere in which, as we know, the sober intoxication of the Spirit, the blessed and burning pain of love for God, and the uncanniness of death with the crucified and godforsaken one can take place. They will look upon the One whom they have pierced and feel the wounds that this pierced One has inflicted on them, right where it touches them most intimately. Then they will recoil in terror from the sleepy routine of being a Church functionary. Fear of being untrue to their true vocation and grace will pierce their hearts. They will flee to Him who alone is our hope and our future. They will pray: "Lord, through your heart, make me through your grace the person with the pierced heart who alone can be your priest."

—*Servants of the Lord,* 108–19

4

Church, Creativity, and Process

"If these persons, in faith and in prayer, in hope and in love, turn to their Lord, the Son of Man, in order to find in him the image after which they themselves are created and toward which they are called..." For Rahner, our relationship to Jesus should disclose something new, something creative within our very selves — something that can be discovered only in relationship with the unique Jesus, but something too that is unique to us. No one else is called to quite the same quality of relationship as I am; no one else has been called to participate in God's life in quite the way that I have.

Rahner's late masterpiece, Foundations of Christian Faith, contains — inevitably — an extensive discussion of Christology. Toward the end of it, there is a highly charged passage,[1] even though it is expressed "with a certain discretion and certain reserve." It is concerned with "the Christian's personal relationship to Jesus Christ." Rahner insists that this theme belongs to theology; it should not be consigned to a pious intellectual ghetto called "the study of spirituality" or "the study of mysticism." "A person is always a Christian in order to become one." Christianity

---

1. Foundations of Christian Faith, 305–7.

... is not just an abstract theory, something that is thought
of as operating objectively, ultimately in the end like a
thing — something to which one subsequently also adopts
a personal attitude. In reality, Christianity understands itself, in its most proper identity, as something that occurs
existentially. ...

We receive the truth of the gospel not once and for all, but
rather as something that we still have

... to be catching up with, and to be bringing to a radical expression through the commitment of our whole lived
existence — throughout the whole length and breadth and
depth of our lives.

For Rahner, Christ's resurrection assures us that the Reign of
God has begun; but the building still has to be continued, in the
darkness of faith, and in ever new ways (for we are called to be
ourselves under God, not some kind of spiritual clone of Christ
or of heroic figures in the tradition). It is on this theme that this
last and longest chapter of selections centers.

It is significant that Rahner's most fully worked-out writings
on the Church occur, not in the context of ecclesiology, not expressly as theology of the Church, but rather in pieces offered
as a "foundation-laying" (Grundlegung) for practical theology
(just as — for him — talk of the divine and human natures hypo-
statically united in Christ is only a framework within which can
take place what really matters: the kind of commitment symbolized in Sacred Heart devotion). Theology and spirituality are
primarily about the God who is continuing to act now, in ways
that are in principle new and unpredictable. Bible and tradition assure us that God is present; they offer, however, no direct
guidance as to how God is present with us, except perhaps by
holding us open to the possibility that this presence may be of a
new, unexpected kind, subverting convention.

The first extract in this chapter is a difficult passage, and some readers may prefer to come back to it later. It brings out how the assurance we have from the resurrection of Christ must be carried over into the community that witnesses it, while nevertheless spelling out quite clearly what membership of that community means: a sharing in the conscious immediacy to God that faith in Christ makes possible for us, an immediacy to which we are faithful not primarily by obeying rules, but rather by being open to a permanent process of change, even revolution (after all, Rahner did publish this material in the mid 1960s).

CHURCH, INSTITUTION, AND SPIRIT

God in person gives God's own self to human beings. God — just God and nothing other. And this self-gift (which is still within history and therefore a matter of faith and hope, not of the immediacy of eternal life in which, as beings whose selves have come to perfection, we will possess the gift in its perfect state) has definitively taken place in Jesus Christ; its acceptance continues in a way that cannot be revoked; it has an abiding and historical, identifiable, and social presence; it can be made known. And just this is what Church is: the abidingness of the accepted Christ in his significance as the definitive self-gift and self-promise of God to humanity. And so the Church truly acts as itself only where, and only insofar as, humanity — in it and through it — is open to God, just as God exists both as God's own self and as God for us: the absolute, nameless mystery, uncircumscribed, unconstrained by norms, and in its lying past all definition the ground and the depth, the norm and source of all things at once. God as God, the God who is God, becomes present in the Church: the living God, the one who destroys any ultimacy held by something you could point to or manage, or by any of the idolatries with their many "gods" (and these do not need any outward images — they can be pursued very "spiritually").

In its very self, therefore, the Church is the institution which militates against any merely institutional reality claiming somehow to stand in the place of God or to represent God. If "revolution" means the militant refusal to assign any ultimate status to a particular, limited reality, then the Church is continual revolution. For in the end its only task is to give glory to God and to save human beings. And to save them by constantly driving them out of their limitations and boundaries into surrender to God — God whom you hold as the true God only as the one to be confessed (in real life, not just in words) as exalted beyond all measure above anything else that exists or that we can conceive. There is therefore a new way in which God makes our transcendence toward Him transcendence toward a mystery that is beyond our own control, a mystery beyond disposal and control that is disposing over us and controlling us. That it remains this permanent revolution, this destruction of the idols, and that it does not ultimately confuse its "religion business" with God's own self (its intrinsic temptation) — that is a permanent miracle of grace, a miracle that is promised to it, and that it is constantly surprised to be discovering.

But it makes this discovery only so as to turn it back on itself as critique, trustfully conscious that this critique of how in practice it expresses itself is an aspect of its very identity: it lies within itself and requires no horizon outside itself, because God's own self, the infinite horizon of critique, is given to it in grace, a grace one of whose forms is self-criticism. The Church confesses the God-human as the presence of God because it understands humanity (through the power of its transcendence liberated by grace) as what supersedes any idol. It adores: adores through acts of faith (it gets beyond using its own present state as a criterion that it can just manipulate);

adores through acts of hope (it moves beyond the present into the unknown future of God, as the one past all grasp); adores through acts of love (it trusts in God's radical past-all-graspness as a gift of the divine love, and accepts it deep within). And only in the devotion of this adoration does it know *whom* it is adoring, since God is only *in this way* present as the ineffable one. [...]

The Church is always aware of its permanent identity on the basis of the divine law determining its existence and how it is constituted. Moreover, in every decision it reflects to a certain extent on its identity as something already given to it, which is both a norm and a limit for this decision. But it would be theological rationalism and ahistorical thinking to hold that this normative reflection on its identity might present the Church with this identity it has in abstract purity, or that this identity could be known without reference to a historically conditioned form. In this form the identity is indeed itself seen, but in such a way that the pure identity in itself and the particular form the identity takes cannot be fully separated when we reflect on them.

Every reflection on metaphysics, indeed precisely when it distinguishes between what is identity and what is the particular form taken by that identity in a construction valid up till now, is itself once again a historical event. This kind of insight about identity is focusing on a *new* form that the identity is taking, a new form arising historically, a form in which the identity can be known and from which a critique of the past can happen. So a specific decision made by the Church to realize its identity in a particular way may well be accompanied by reflection on its identity and based on that reflection, but the particular decision with its specific content, whether understood as a matter of duty or just as a matter of what is permissible, cannot be strictly deduced simply from this knowledge of its identity. This is because, as we have said, this awareness of identity cannot escape how it has been shaped historically.

It follows that the process leading to a decision can never include explicitly a complete certainty as to whether it has been made on the basis of the metaphysical identity or from its specific, historical form; or from legitimate or illegitimate actual forms. And second, the historical form of a personal identity — and therefore also of the Church — is always (because it is free, and historically quite individual, even in the form it takes in time) something "one and only," something that cannot be deduced. And so the balance at specific points in history between preservation of the old and a new realization of the identity that is a critique of what has simply been there historically — this is something that can never fully be a matter of reflection. Thus practical theology is a discipline that can only approach its goal ever more closely; it never "gets there." It is also an attempt — you cannot avoid this, however unwelcome you may find it — at answering a charismatic imperative. It is in a space where it can no longer accreditate itself just from the abstract concepts of theology, but only by appeal to the charismatic "instinct" of other members of the Church and of the Church's leadership, and at the same time also by inviting people to trust that God's Spirit is present to the Church precisely where it can no longer reflectively assure itself that its decisions are correct.

— *Theology of Pastoral Action*, 31–32, 58

One consequence of this vision of how God deals with the world is that spirituality, in a real sense, is the source of theology. There is a life of the Spirit that theology cannot fully regulate or anticipate. This is the starting point of Rahner's difficult, in some ways wrong-headed, but nevertheless seminally creative theological study of Ignatius and the Spiritual Exercises, published in 1956.

THEOLOGY AND
THE LIFE OF THE SPIRIT

It would not be unfair, in my opinion, to the achievements of the major commentators on St. Ignatius's Exercises to hold that a proper theology of the Exercises is still something to be desired — and that the satisfaction of this need, in the way we inevitably want today, is still a task outstanding. Even if we supposed that the major commentators of past centuries had done enough for their own time, it still remains the case that every age must think through classic works like the *Spiritual Exercises* anew, from its own standpoint. [...]

We need to begin by breaking with a habit, doing away with an emotional attitude: the habit of thinking that when we are dealing with books like this that have changed the world, we are in fact only dealing with pious things that can be taken for granted — things that, though very useful for leading a devout life, have no potential to stimulate theologians. For, after all, everything that is said in such edifying books theologians have known for ages, even if they might be inclined, gently and kindly, to concede that this matter in such books is said in ways that are very nice, psychologically effective, edifying, and practical.

But it is not like this at all. Of course there is "spiritual literature" available to all and sundry that is derivative from high theology in the sense that it just repeats in simplified fashion what is already in academic theological books. But there is also a kind of "spiritual reading" that has a different relationship to learned theology. This goes beyond Holy Scripture and the pronouncements of the Church's teaching office. There is a "spiritual literature" that is *prior* to the kind of reflection that theology does, that is more fundamental, that is wiser and more experienced than the wisdom of the classroom — a literature in which the faith of the Church, the Word of God, and the work of the Holy Spirit (who never ceases to be at work in the Church) are expressed in a more fundamental way than in theological monographs. There is a "spiritual literature" that is not just mining nuggets from theology for ordinary devout people, that is not mining nuggets from the faith of the Church and the Word of God in such a way that the nuggets could, in fact, be predicted by anyone interested and clever enough. On the contrary, it represents "creative," "primordial" ways of appropriating the revelation of God in Christ: as the gift of ancient Christianity is being given in a new way to a new time through the Spirit of God, so this new appropriation is happening in a way that sets a pattern, that befits the time, and that is a generative model.

To do justice to the significance of such books, you obviously need to have a feel for how an idea's after-effects and influence are one thing, and its initial discovery in creative originality quite another. However obvious and illuminating such an idea may appear later, its first clear arrival is nevertheless always a miracle of the Spirit of God in history, who has His times and His prophets — prophets carved out of a wood very different from that of their disciples and of those who sit on professorial chairs. One must have a feel for how it is almost inevitably the fate of such primordial knowledge to be watered down and rendered innocuous as, with the best intentions, it is expurgated for popularization, so that what began as a great light becomes a candle, cozily illuminating Mr. Average's tiny room. The *Spiritual Exercises* fall within *this* kind of "spiritual literature." [...]

To make the Exercises an object of theology in this sort of way, in other words to ask questions as theologians about them in order to explain them as something from which you *learn*, rather than just explaining them in terms of what you know quite independently of them — this is very difficult for theologians. For the Exercises speak in a language that, frankly, provokes the theologians' arrogance, so that they find nothing behind the text other than what people already know, and at best just think that there are poorly expressed, obscure places in the text that need to be illuminated through their own theological wisdom.

Let us be honest, we who are theologians. When we hear the old tradition that the Exercises arose from a quite special impulse given by the Holy Spirit, then either we believe it in a way that is fundamentally false, or we cut this claim down so that it does not threaten us. We can think that the actual miracle of this book consists in the fact that a person who had not yet studied theology did not run up against theological problems; besides he used very practically and skillfully — amazingly skillfully, that we grant — what he fundamentally knew from us, even if only through the tiny channel of the catechism and other edifying literature. But if we once accept that there are books in Christianity, that there are books that are not deducible (however much they draw life from what has been handed down, and indeed in one way only want to say this again), that are truly the miracle of a specific and yet truly new realization of the Christian identity that is always the same — then the position that theology takes up regarding this book will be different.

A theology of this sort of Christianity really can be written. Or at least something like this can be on our agenda. And it can begin only by subverting the appearance of something obvious and boringly conventional, by asking questions that do not go out into the world with the answer already tied up inside them. If, then, some questions (by no means all the questions) are put here that the Exercises, when taken seriously, put to the theologian, then sympathetic readers should not understand this as idle subtlety, nor complain that the proper answer does not come at once. Rather they should do just one thing: take the Exercises seriously, and not begin from a tacit prejudice to the

effect that nothing more could possibly be in the Exercises than
what theoretical theology has worked out ages ago.
                              — *The Dynamic Element in the Church*, 84–89

*We always need to be careful when we hear it said that a
theologian is a holy man, that a theology is somehow "spiritual," or "nourished by prayer," or "in living contact with
spirituality." At its worst, such talk is manipulative: an attempt
to pass off a shoddy argument or a conventional position as
valid by exploiting people's trust and good will. More often,
it undermines speculative thinking: the pious imagination can
seize on an image like that of Rahner praying the rosary on a
public platform and reassure itself that theology is fundamentally harmless, that it will not change anything. Rahner thinks
"spirituality" important for rather different reasons. It is not
that Rahner brought theology back into contact with "spirituality"; rather, he saw the two as fundamentally identical. The
study of theology just is the study of God's continuing dealings
with humanity. And the importance of "prayer" in theology
is not a matter of any hare-brained belief that piety can substitute for serious thinking, nor of reassurance for the devout
that theology is not after all so threatening. Prayer is important for theology because the living contact with God that it
betokens is an absolutely vital source for theology, one that
should be moving us beyond the conventional and familiar into
something new.*

*Not, of course, that this living contact is confined to "prayer,"
or even to the experience of believing Christians. Rahner was not
the sort of theologian who wrote much about literature or art,
and when he tried the results were usually not very successful.
But this deeply felt "Prayer for the Creative" — originally written
for a youth arts festival in 1954 — nevertheless brings out the
importance of human creativity in Rahner's spiritual vision.*

PRAYER FOR THE CREATIVE

Eternal God, creator of all humanity and all things, visible and invisible, God of all history — Lord and goal, strength and light of all people, we make our prayers today for all who create culture.

Lord, who is there already praying for them? Yet we know that you will their goal and their creative power, their toil and their productions. For you will humanity in the full, ever new, unfolding of its identity; you will human beings that become the work of their own hands. You love the persons who realize their own identity through their work, and thus express the identity that is an image and likeness of your own glory. And only with their grace can they be what they are meant to be according to your will, Father of poets, primordial source of all life, spirit of all true inspiration.

And so we pray to you and call down your Holy Spirit on them. Awaken among us people of creative power: thinkers, poets, artists. We need them. For them too the word is still valid about how humanity starves if all it has is bread for the body, and if the Word that comes from your mouth is not its nourishment. Give these young people courage to obey their vocation, to carry the burden and the pain of such a call, not to betray this enjoined task to the addiction of money and cheap applause from superficial people who just want to be entertained. If, because they are proclaimers, they can say what humanity is through word and image, through tone and gesture, then let them say *the whole of this*. Give them the experience of humanity not as a locked-in hell of its own nothingness, but as the fair, blessed land over which the heaven of your own endlessness and freedom stands. They do not need always to be talking about you; they should refer to you by your name only when they are filled with the breath of purest bliss or of ultimate pain. Otherwise they should honor you with silence. Otherwise they should extol the earth and humanity. But at the same time, they should be silently bearing you in their hearts, you from whom their work springs. Then even the tiniest song is an echo of the joy in your heaven, and their account of the darkest depths is still embraced by your mercy, and by a yearning for light, justice, and eternal love. Then even the attempt to speak is a reflection of the gentle patience with which you love us in our daily drudge.

Give them the courage for light and for joy. In the darkness of this time, given the meager poverty of our hearts, *this* sort of courage is grace *from you*. But give it them, because we need such high courage. Give them the courage to be discriminating and to be decisive. There's no need for them to rationalize too much. But their works should help people see that an integrated heart has created them, a heart open to all things that nevertheless is seeing you in all things and all things in you and is not touched by cowardly peace between the good and the bad, the light and the darkness. Given them courage to keep on beginning again, because only that way will they find their origin in what has been true from the very beginning. Make them say what *your* spirit has given them in their hearts, not what the powers stuffed with mediocrity want to hear. If they experience life's vanity and emptiness, the breakdown of their creativity, if they find the times they live in unreceptive, let them even then still believe that in your sight what is vain is never in vain, that you have taken delight as you have seen their work and received their breaking hearts gently within your own.

Your eternal Word, the reflection of your being and the image of your glory, has in person come into our flesh, has accepted all that is human as *his own*. With greater expressiveness and greater love than any other creator, he has placed his own heart right within the image made by his hand, so that humanity itself can be the expression and image of his glory. And therefore, whether people know it or not, every cultural creation is a piece of your Word's own history, because everything has become his own world, into which he came so as to live with it, suffer with it, and transfigure it with himself — and this Word of yours will never again, right into eternity, be without it.

Let those for whom we are praying understand this. What they are creating is inevitably either a piece of the cross to which people guiltily nail your Son, and thus their judgment; or else it is part of the coming of your Son's eternal Kingdom, and thus their grace. For this Kingdom is not coming just from outside, as an end to this world, a judgment on it. It is coming as the secret grace out from within the center of this earthly reality, since your eternal Word, descending into his creation, has become the heart of all things. And thus everything they create can and must be a promise, that your eternal Kingdom is coming, the Kingdom of truth and love, the Kingdom that transfigures the whole human being, body and soul, earth and heaven. So make them heralds, multipliers of this Kingdom, into which, transformed and transfigured, everything that humanity has formed through partaking in your creative power will be preserved for eternity. May the Spirit of your Son come over them, so that your name may be praised, now in this age, and in the eternity of eternities. Amen.

The next seven extracts are all concerned with the Church. For Rahner, the Church is part and parcel of the life of grace. The self-gift of God that we call grace, made definitively and irrevocably manifest in the Risen Christ, is located in a human community. Because grace is God's self-gift to humanity, it makes no sense to suppose we can experience grace as something that frees us from the messy business of trying to relate to other people. But this account of why the Church is indispensable to the spiritual life is importantly different from the mindless, uncritical loyalty that immature authority often demands. Because the Church is drawing us into the life of God's own self, in a constant, living process, it also empowers

*its members to be critical, both of themselves and of the
institution.*

*The following two pieces, one from the 1930s, one from the
1980s, bring out how Rahner's unquestioning commitment to
the Church could stand alongside a righteous frustration with
Church authority.*

GOD OF LAW

In my life, are you the Spirit of freedom or the God of Laws?
Or are you both? Or are you the God of freedom through the
law? Your laws, which you yourself have given, are not chains.
Your own commands are commands of freedom — that is true.
In their sharp realism and remorselessness, they free me from a
dull sinking into my own narrowness, with its wretched, cowardly desires. They awaken a freedom for the love of you. They
are truth, because they command us to put first things first, to
give priority to what is from above — and not to raise what is
paltry to the altars of our own lives. And because they are truth,
they are liberating, these commands that you yourself gave in
the new covenant — or rather made over to us, when Christ
set us free for freedom (Gal. 5:1), and when thus nothing else
remained for us except the law of freedom (James 2:12).

Your own commandments may be heavy, but they are liberating. But, Lord, what about the commandments that are given
by human beings, given in your name? Permit me for once, God
of freedom and honest speaking, to express freely what can go
through my heart in grumpy, grumbling moments — for, after
all, you hear such thoughts kindly. Lord, you got rid of the
old law "that neither our ancestors nor we have been able to
bear" (Acts 15:10). But you have also appointed authorities in
this world — secular authorities and principally spiritual ones.
And sometimes it seems to me that they have been busily filling

in the holes that your Spirit of freedom had torn out from the fences of laws and directives in the Pentecost storm. There are the 2,414 paragraphs of the *Code of Canon Law*.[2] But — drat it — not even these were enough: how many *responsa* have already been added to make the canon lawyers happy. And the couple of thousand liturgical decrees also demand our observance. To be able to praise you in the breviary in "psalms and hymns and spiritual songs," to sing and make melody to you in my heart (Eph. 5:19), I have to have a map, a *Directory,* that has to be printed in a new form every year — so complicated is this praise of God. And there is an *Official Bulletin* in the Kingdom of your Holy Spirit, and innumerable bundles of records, questions, answers, reports, decisions, meetings, precedents, instructions from the many congregations and commissions. And is there any limit to the power of moral theologians to ask fiddly questions, until all the decrees of every authority are put in order and interpreted. And how gloriously complicated a calculation the giving of indulgences has become! Even a short while ago, learned theologians were arguing whether a sick person needed to kiss the image of your Son on the cross fourteen times, six times, or fewer.

In their great zeal, your servants and administrators have left nothing unthought through, nothing undecreed during this long time in which you, having traveled into the silent distances of eternity, have been pleased to entrust your house to your servants. But "where the Spirit of the Lord is, there is freedom," your word says. I don't want to complain against these prudent and faithful servants whom you have placed over your workers. To their credit, I want to let you know that normally the charge that your Son once made against the scribes and the Pharisees who sit on Moses' seat (Matt. 23:2) does not apply to

---

2. Rahner is, of course, referring to the 1917 *Code of Canon Law,* which has now been superseded by the 1983 *Code.*

them. They have laid the heavy burdens that they tie not only on others, but also on themselves.

—from *Encounters with Silence,* 36–37

FOR THE CHURCH

I'm meant to pray for the Church, my God. Indeed I do so, every day, at the celebration of the Lord's Supper. After all, my faith can live only in the community of those who together form the holy Church of Jesus. And therefore it is (along with much else) indispensable for my salvation that the Church really can be the home and foundation of my faith. Of course I know that the Church is always this for me and can always be so, through the power of your irrevocable grace. But because it is also the Church of wretched sinners, it can vary in *how far* it is the foundation and home of my faith. It can make it both easier and more difficult for me to believe in you and your victorious love for me.

I really don't think I'm better than other people in the Church. I know that I myself am anything but brilliantly shining evidence for the origin of the Church in God's grace-giving will: I, who am after all a member of this Church and am supposed to represent it. But that enables me also to say that my sisters and brothers in this Church often disturb me when I'm meant to be praying, "I believe in one, holy, catholic, and apostolic Church, the communion of saints," and on that basis "the life of the world to come." How boring, antiquated, bothered only with the system's good repute — how short-sighted, how addicted to power the "office-holders" in the Church seem to me: how conservative in a bad sense and clericalist. And when they are unctuous with it, when they parade their good will and selflessness, then it gets even harder, because I hardly ever hear them confessing publicly and clearly their mistakes and ineptitudes. They want us to believe in their infallibility today and forget what appalling mistakes they've made in the past, the important things that they didn't do. How often they get themselves worked up in holy indignation about some deed or other; their holy anger about the social order that is the ultimate cause for the wrong action I sense less clearly. They moralize a lot; but of the passion of joy about the message of your grace in which you give yourself — a passion overflowing the whole mind and heart — there is normally far less to be felt. And yet their moral sermons would stand much more chance of being heard if there were so much as a small passing reference to the praise of your glorious grace, the overflowing fullness of life that you want to impart to us.

The official pomposities of your Church that often seem to me so arthritically and decadently European, as if the Church were not the world Church but a European Church with exports throughout the world — all that's beyond my even wanting to talk about it. Three hundred years ago people in our part of the world burned witches, and it could turn out very badly for you if you questioned whether witches existed. Today this mass frenzy no longer exists in the Church — yet do we know for certain that there aren't other forms of mass frenzy around in which the Church is naively colluding? Among those who took part in the frenzy back then, there were holy, learned, and devout folk of good will who failed to see how much their actions contradicted the gospel of Jesus. Can we say in advance that today's Church is immune from all such horrors? How might I come to know this? How could you prove that there was such an immunity?

My God, have mercy upon us poor, narrow-minded, sinful fools, on us who form the body of Your Church. Have mercy upon those who call themselves your representatives (to be honest, I don't think this word is a good one, because God surely cannot be represented). Have mercy upon us. I don't want to be one of those who find fault with the officeholders in the Church

and then contribute all the more to your Church's lack of credibility. Still less do I want to be one of those who are stupid
enough to wonder whether they still want to remain in the
Church. I want to keep on working for the clear-sightednesss
that can see the miracles of your grace that even today occur in
the Church. I must confess that I see these miracles more plainly
among the young people in the Church (Andrea, for instance,
who during her studies did the washing for a whole year in a
home for abandoned young people)[3] than among the great ones
in the Church, for whom — and this is inevitable — it is also
quite cushy in secular society. But perhaps my eyes are dim, and
I've got an emotional problem with "authority" and "power."

There are hymns that we can sing quite properly in praise of
the holy Church. After all, it professes your grace throughout all
times, and proclaims that you are ineffably exalted over everything that is conceivable apart from you. And therefore it will
live until the end of time — even if then I await the Kingdom
of God that will abolish even the Church. But even a somewhat
bitter lament and a plea for God's mercy on the Church are
nevertheless praising this Church and your mercy.

— from *Prayers of a Lifetime*, 114–17

*Rahner was, nevertheless, deeply at home in the Church. The
next extract is a long one, and its length contributes to its effect.
Written — so archival evidence tells us — during the war for
young men at an improvised, clandestine seminary in Vienna, it*

---

3. Andrea Tafferner, author of a distinguished doctorate on Rahner's moral theology and now a professor of theology at a Catholic Institute in Münster, who has
kindly supplied to me the information that follows.

The home Rahner refers to was founded in the early 1980s by Fr. Georg
Sporschill, who was also at that stage editor of a journal and managed to extract from Rahner most of the valuable late pieces in this collection. Rahner joined
in many of the house's activities, even joining in a Mass in a prison. Rahner es-
teemed this experimental project highly: in that it enabled committed young people
to live in solidarity with the marginalized. He thought that the project represented
an authentic style of ecclesial belonging, and he supported the house with his
friendship.

*meditates on the different steps of the rite of priestly ordination,
as performed before the Council. There is an intensity of feeling,
an innocence of commitment, that shines through this writing
and can still touch even those of us whom Rahner's own theology has taught to feel quite uncomfortable with the hierarchical
symbolisms of a modern Roman Catholic ordination.*

PRAYER ON THE EVE OF ORDINATION

The Presentation of the Candidates

Tomorrow, my God, it will be said: "Holy Mother Church asks
that you ordain these deacons here present to the burden of the
priesthood."

So this is something your Church wants. You in your Church.
I have not chosen you; you have chosen me. How blessed is this
choice because it is your choice, the choice of your unfathomable ways that are love and compassion. How terrifying is this
choice because it is your choice, you who choose in the sovereign freedom and serenity of your ruling, you who choose the
weak for something beyond the human, the least for what is
greatest, so that none may boast, but rather God's power alone
be made perfect in our weakness.

O have me know that your word, "my yoke is easy, and my
burden is light," holds good of the "burden of the priesthood"
too, so that the crushing burden of your priesthood's cross may
become for me God's blessed burden, the abundant burden of
every grace.

And then I shall hear the bishop's question: "Do you know
them to be worthy?" My God, who is worthy of you? Who is
worthy of you? Nothingness worthy before your sovereign being? Sinfulness worthy before your all-consuming sanctity? Lo,
I must pray with Isaiah as he was called to be a prophet and

heard the "Holy, holy, holy" of the adoring seraph: "Woe is me! I am lost, for I am a man of unclean lips, and I live among a people of unclean lips."

But you make me worthy, because your call, your grace and strength are my worthiness, and because I, despite my "Lord, I am not worthy," can, since Isaiah, boldly and confidently say, "I am here" — "here I am; send me."

The Laying On of Hands

And then the bishop will lay his hands on my head, in silence — and in this silence, as on a Christmas Eve or Holy Saturday — "while gentle silence envelops all things" — your almighty Word and the fire of your Spirit will transform me into a priest of your Son, my Lord. Your Spirit will come down upon me, the gift of God's grace, which is not a spirit of cowardice, but rather a spirit of power and of love and of self-discipline (2 Tim. 1:7), the spirit that makes priests, people of sacrifice and witnesses of your Word, the Spirit that tears us away from ourselves and takes our lives into the sacrifice of Christ, offering them along with his for the salvation of the world.

The bishop will lay his hands on me as in the Old Covenant hands were laid on the scapegoat, the sacrifice that atoned for sin. For I am to follow him whom you, when he "knew no sin," made to be sin for our sake (2 Cor. 5:21), so that in him we might have a part in the righteousness of God. I am to follow the Lamb of God who took the world's sin upon Himself (John 1:29), upon whom you have laid the iniquity of us all (Isa. 53:6). As Moses appointed Joshua leader of the people by laying hands on him, and he was "full of the spirit of wisdom, for Moses had laid his hands on him" (Deut. 34:9); as the Levites were appointed by the laying on of hands (Num. 8:10); as Jesus laid his hands on children and on the sick; as the Apostles laid hands on their own disciples when they sent them out, and set them apart for the work to which your Spirit had called them — laid hands, so that their spirit would pass on to others (Acts 13:2–3).

The bishop will lay his hands on me, and I shall be taken into the ranks of your servants who for two thousand years have been making their way through all ages and all lands, declaring your name before kings and nations. Into the unbroken chain that you began when your Son, our Lord, said, "Go into all the world...see, I am with you"; into the unbroken chain of mission, of labor in a common destiny, of a new strength and power; into the one sacred race of Your priests that is renewed eternally not by blood and the will of the flesh but by birth from the Spirit and from the power of Your command; into the unbroken chain of Your priestly race that will never die out until you come to judge the living and the dead.

The bishop will lay his hands on me. And then, still silent, he will take them from my head. But your hand, O my God, will still remain upon me.

Your hands will remain upon me.

The hands of the Almighty, gentler than a mother's hands.

The hands that have created and sustained all things.

The hands that can weigh heavy on a person and will often weigh me down during my priestly life.

The hands that strike and heal.

The hands of the living God into which it is a dreadful thing to fall.

The hands into which at death I shall commend my spirit.

When your hand rests upon me through the bishop's hand, and so also your Spirit, then the prophecy of Isaiah will apply to me: "The spirit of the Lord GOD is upon me, because the LORD has anointed me; he has sent me to bring good news to the oppressed, to bind up the brokenhearted, to proclaim liberty to the captives, and release to the prisoners; to proclaim the year of the Lord's favor." Then I shall be able to say with

Jesus, "Today this Scripture has been fulfilled in your hearing"
(Luke 4:21).

Tomorrow, as it was already for Timothy, my confreres, my
comrades in the army of the Lord will fraternally lay their hands
on me so that one Spirit and one power and one mission may
live and work in all of us, so that the priestly spirit of Jesus'
Church may be engendered yet further. Then we shall belong
to the presbyterate; we will have grown to the point that we
belong with the Elders. On us the responsibility will then rest
to see that the Spirit of the apostles and martyrs, the faithful, strong, selfless, believing, self-sacrificing Spirit, the valiant,
daring, cheerful Spirit — that this Spirit does not die out.

The Investiture

Then the bishop will cross the stole over my breast, over my
heart, and clothe me with the vestment of a priest, the chasuble.
You, my God, in addition to my baptismal robe, give me also
my priestly vestment. Have me bring both spotless to your judgment seat! Before you I am of myself stark naked, for who, in
the sight of your incorruptible justice, is anything but nothingness and sin? But clothe me with the garment of justice and holy
discipline; clothe me, the prodigal son, in the garments of your
grace, of light, of everlasting clarity. And give me as well the
armor of light (Rom. 13:12), so that I may be girded with truth,
carrying the breastplate of righteousness, shod with readiness to
proclaim the gospel of peace, armed with the shield of faith, the
helmet of salvation, and the sword of God's Word (see Eph. 6).

The Anointing

Then the bishop will anoint my hands with the sign of the cross
and bind them.

The hands that are to bless.

The hands that are to bestow God's peace on sinners.

The hands that will be extended in prayer for God's holy people.

The hands that are to hold the Lord's body and blood.

"Filling a man's hand," was already in the Old Covenant an expression that meant ordaining him a priest. Fill my hands with your blessing. Let them never be empty. Let them always be sanctified. Let them always be nimble in your service and bound to your command. Let them never reach out to evil. Let your cross, emblem of your love, burn always on my hands like scars, so that I too may always bear on my body the Stigmata of Christ. Let me be anointed, as you anointed Aaron and his priests to your royal priesthood, as you anointed kings, as you anointed prophets to be *your* prophets. Let me be anointed like your anointed one, the Messiah, our Lord, with the oil of gladness beyond all my companions, with the oil of strength and holiness, with the oil of the Holy Spirit, the oil of the godhead. With the anointing that abides in us, that teaches us about all things (1 John 2:27).

The Presentation of the Paten and Chalice

Then for the first time the bishop will entrust the paten and the chalice with the offertory gifts to my anointed hands. "I will take the cup of salvation and call upon the name of the Lord." I shall hold the paten that is to bear the Lord's body. I shall grasp the chalice that contains within itself the ransom for the sins of the world. I shall be Your priest. Tomorrow and every day of my life I shall celebrate the sacrifice of Christ. I shall be empowered with the word that transforms the world into God. I shall offer the never-ending sacrifice of the new and eternal covenant. I shall hold in my hands the body that was delivered up for us. I shall lift up the chalice with the blood that was poured out for me and for all, so that we could be redeemed and sanctified in the truth. I shall give my sisters and brothers your body, the sacrament of grace, the sacrament of the Lord's death, the sacrament of unity and love, the sacrament of the new body and of the resurrection. I and my whole life shall be drawn into your death. I shall be your priest.

Then, Lord Jesus Christ, eternal priest, you will stand before me and look at me as you looked at your Apostles, with a look of one who knows all things, of one who is love without origin, and say to me too: "Now I shall not call you servants, but my friends. I have called you friends, because I have made known to you everything that I have heard from my Father" (John 15:15). Lord, I am your servant and the son of your handmaid. I am your friend because you have said that I am, and your word is effective, almighty. I am your friend because you have given me all that you have — your Father, your life, your grace, your command, your authority, your lot, your cross, your death, and your eternal victory. And to my holy exuberance you speak once again, realistically: "You are my friends if you do what I command you."

The Creed

And then I shall say the Creed once more, the "good confession in the presence of many witnesses" that already Timothy was making (1 Tim. 6:13). The creed of the Apostles and of my ancestors and of my parents. The creed of my childhood faith, familiar and beloved. The creed that gave joy to my youth, that I have stood by as a man, that is better than all the wisdom of the world — the creed that is God's word enduring forever. The creed to which my word, my labor, and my blood now belong — the creed that I am to speak and to live.

The Commission to Bind and Loose

And once more the bishop will his lay hands on me and tell me that I am sent to bind and to loose, to judge and to forgive in your name. Have me always love this quiet, grave, humble office of sin being forgiven. This office of the ultimate and bitter gravity in human life: sin. This office of your inexhaustible mercy and forbearance. This office in which your justice and your mercy become one, most humane humanity and most divine godliness. This office of silence and patience. This office of eternal life.

The Promise of Obedience

And finally the bishop will take my hands in his hands, and I shall promise the Church obedience and loyalty: exacting and faithful obedience, selfless obedience, obedience whereby persons forget their own life and pour it into a task that is greater than themselves, only to find themselves again in this steadfastness and constant generosity. See, I lay my hands in your hands, my God. So take my hands, then, and lead me: through joy and grief, through honor and disgrace, in labor and pain, in the daily drudge and in great moments, in the holy silence of your house but also on the long, dusty streets of the world. Lead me today and always, lead me into the kingdom of Your eternal life.

After I have been in this way called by you, raised up by you, anointed with power by you, sent out by you, I shall arise and go away again as your priest, your anointed one, your messenger, your witness, as your priest for all eternity. Ordination to the priesthood is really your final great word spoken into my life, Your last, decisive, definitive, irrevocable call. A call that shapes my life now forever. Whatever happens in my life now can only be just the effect, the living out of this final and definitive call, only just the carrying out of this one ultimate command that will now forever shape my life. Grant, therefore, that I may be found faithful. You have called me; you will also bring it to completion (1 Thess. 5:24). For your gifts are given unrepentantly. On the day of my ordination let the morning prayer of my priestly life be these words from the spirit of Ignatius, the holy warrior:

> Dearest Lord, teach me to be generous:
> teach me to serve You as You deserve:
> to give and not to count the cost,
> to fight and not to heed the wounds,
> to toil and not to seek for rest,
> to labor and not to ask for reward
> save that of knowing I am doing your will. Amen.[4]

The older Rahner could never have written anything as unctuous as that prayer (though he was quite happy to publish it in the 1960s). But the sense of belonging it evinces remained with him throughout his life. One of Rahner's most attractive books is called Mein Problem, *and it was subtitled, "Karl Rahner answers young people."[5] In his old age Rahner visited the youth group in a Vienna parish and gave a talk. Afterward, twenty-four of them wrote him letters about questions they had — not simply religious ones. The book brings together these letters with*

---

4. This text is attributed to Ignatius and certainly reflects important aspects of his spirituality. But it was not written by him, and its origin is unknown — not unlike the prayer, "Lord, make me an instrument of your peace," attributed to Francis of Assisi.

5. There was a U.S. American translation done in 1984 by Dimension Books, Denville, New Jersey. It is particularly difficult to capture the spontaneity of letters in a translation, and this effort is not terribly successful. Whereas the original had an expressive picture of inquiring young people on the cover, the U.S. publication was called, portentously, *Is Christian Life Possible Today?* and was subtitled *Questions and Answers on the Fundamentals of Christian Life*. The cover had a rather bad picture of Rahner on his own. The youth group in question was run by the energetic Fr. Sporschill.

Rahner's answers. The young people's directness is matched by Rahner being able to draw on his own theology to address their issues with a real respect and seriousness. There is perhaps no better witness to how Rahner's own theology seeks to respond to basic human experience.

TO LOVE GOD
I DON'T NEED ANY CHURCH

Dear Fr. Rahner:

It's best for me to begin quite directly. After a lot of thought, I believe in God but not in the Church. Why it's not easy to say. Partly because the Church in my view has got a shady past (look at the Middle Ages), partly because I can come closer to God even without the Church and can pray to God even without the Mass, and for me this gets more easily to the goal. It almost makes me sick to look at people grinding out the prayers they've learned by heart, or that someone leads them in, without paying any attention to the meaning, I find it ridiculous to pray the rosary, because I can't see any point in it except as perhaps a way into the Mass or God. But couldn't you recite a recipe from a cookbook just as well?

I also can't see any point in going to confession, because I don't believe that a priest can forgive me my sins just with a few words and with a prayer as "punishment." That means I can carry on committing sins and then have myself "forgiven." Why shouldn't I also bear the consequences of my sins if I've committed them? Having a human being forgive them is only a sign of fear about coming before God with my sins and really paying for them. But unfortunately I'm not strong enough to pay for them during my life, so I'll have to do it after death.

Besides that I don't agree with all the Church's rituals, because I think someone who really believes doesn't need any symbols for it. I also seem to remember once having read in the Bible that one shouldn't pray publicly at the street corners or in the synagogue, and after this (for me) reassuring word comes the Our Father. This place is the most important for me in the New Testament.

Again, I sometimes think I'm wrong and wonder about what I'm thinking. Then I wish I still had firm faith in God and in the Church. I hope you can help me to understand the Church so that I don't carry on seeing it so negatively. I'd be really interested in what you think about it.

I wait in hope of an answer, and meanwhile send you my very warmest greetings.

Greg

Dear Greg:

I really enjoyed reading your letter, I must admit; at times I laughed at it. If you think that you can just as easily recite a recipe as pray the rosary, then I don't think you have ever prayed the rosary. If you had already tried it more often, perhaps it might have struck you that even the monotony of this prayer — quite apart from its value precisely as a prayer — contains an enormous power to calm people down, to help them let go, to give them the courage to step aside from everything that goes on in the day and just be themselves. But that's all a side-issue.

Actually I'm quite puzzled by how you young people have such problems with the Church. You're not like us individualists of the past, or at least of an age that is passing. You're inclined to something that one might call — in a certain sense — "socialism." Young people today want a sense of belonging to a community; they demand that we be closer to each other like sisters and brothers; they're keen on service to others. But if a community isn't just going to be an interest group that will soon break up, but really give people a lasting basis for their life, then this kind of structured — indeed we have to say institutional —

community requires individuals to fit in, to be disciplined and selfless.

It's strange for me that you want to be socialists and yet can't make allowances for the Church. But the Church is a community in which, of course, there are duties, rules, and norms, to which you have to fit in with a certain selflessness. And of course it is only when you do this, without reservations and honestly, that you find the blessing that this kind of community can give you. Something similar applies in a family. You can find security and the help you give each other only if you just do without question what this kind of life together inevitably demands. That's how it is in the Church too.

I've often heard people claiming that they can come close to God without the Church: they say they find God in nature and so on. Obviously no Christian can doubt that those who are following their conscience in selfless fidelity are ultimately able to find God. But could it not be that a conscience open to reality, the full range of it, might recognize that the community of the Church is also a demand that God places on us through this conscience? Could it not be that people come more closely and more radically toward the infinite God through the Church and with the Church, or that there are experiences of God that you can have only in the Church?

Is it then really the case that when you live in and with the Church, you can only "grind out" prayers and talk yourself out of your sins in order to get forgiveness? Isn't it that whoever really understands the mystery of the Eucharist in faith experiences a closeness to Christ Jesus, to his life, his death on the cross, and his resurrection that you can't find anywhere else? Can't you join in the assembly of people praying in a genuinely living and personal way?

By all means, normal Christians can seek out a liturgy, a community of prayer, a celebration of the Eucharist that somehow seems closer, that might cause them fewer problems than this or that liturgy in this or that parish. But simply to write off what happens in the Church's liturgy as the ridiculous grinding out of prayers — that's just unfair. Are you really living your own life in such untroubled union and fellowship with the holy God of life eternal that you don't also need Jesus' word of forgiveness for your guilt through the agency of the Church? I have to say honestly that your sentence, "someone who really believes doesn't need any symbols for it," struck me as terribly silly.

Are you a person with body and soul? Surely what goes on in the most intimate center of your personality must inevitably express itself in what the body does. Can you do without art or music? For there what's going on are precisely symbolic actions, and in fact nothing else — through these people express the most intimate things about themselves. Why should it be any different when it comes to our relationship with God? Certainly, demonstrative prayer at a street corner is not one of the necessary and sensible ways in which our relationship to God can be embodied — especially not if this only happens (and this is what Jesus is getting at) in order to parade your piety before others. But to claim that Jesus' word against such parading of piety is the most important word in the New Testament is simply ridiculous. It's also quite clearly against the intention of Jesus, who obviously, like the rest of us, cannot always be saying all that is ultimate and decisive in what motivates him.

When Jesus says we should love God with our whole heart and our whole strength, this is obviously for Jesus a more important word than what you have declared to be the most important word in the New Testament. Of course you could say that the whole of what drives Jesus and what he wants to teach us lies hidden in every word of Jesus, even when they have to be said one by one. But again, that makes no difference to the point that what really matters in Jesus' message is present in different ways and at different levels of intensity, more or less urgently, more or less powerfully.

Of course in what I've just said — to which in a short letter I can't add much more — I've not described what really matters ultimately in the Church. But if people are people, and as such social beings, and if there are people who believe in Jesus as the person through whom alone they ultimately come to God and hear his final Word of salvation, of forgiveness, of grace, and of eternal life, then there has to be a community of those who flock round Jesus: in other words there has to be Church.

The next step is that you have to learn to give — patiently, kindly, readily — and not just take. Then you'll grow into the life of this community of faith. Try it.

You say you would like to believe in the Church as strongly as you believe in God. But in the end there is absolutely no need to have exactly the same faith — that absolute identification of yourself with the other — when it comes to the Church that you have in the case of God. Because the Church isn't God; and the ultimate surrender, the ultimate self-identification demanding our whole being is something we have only in respect of God. But there are other realities besides, different from God and alongside God, toward which our relationship has to be positive, precisely because God wants this. And therefore we can and must seek and find a positive relationship with the Church as well.

Try it and be patient — and be critical about yourself too. Don't regard the experiences of the Church you've had so far as all that there is. It's like what can happen with another person. Your first experiences are less good, and you think that it will always necessarily be like that. Then you slowly realize what a good guy that person is — how helpful, how reliable. It can go that kind of way with the Church too. You yourself say that you sometimes think you are wrong and doubt your own lines of thought. If this is true, then you're actually already on the right road. And it will draw you closer to the Church.

I send you too — as you put it in your letter — my very warmest greetings.

Yours

Karl Rahner

— *Is Christian Life Possible Today?* 45–51

As we said earlier, Rahner developed an understanding of the Church as a foundation for a theology that was essentially practical. He did not expect to be able to solve the problems thrown up by Church living in any theoretical way. Adopting the persona of Ignatius in 1978, he wrote of how difficult it was simultaneously to follow a call to radical discipleship at the margins and to stay in good standing with the hierarchy. Ultimately one has to rely on divine providence:

> *... you must try to bring about the miracle of this double identity over and over again. The sum will never work out. But try for it, over and over again. One of the two on its own is not enough. Only the two together are sufficiently crucifying.* ("Ignatius of Loyola Speaks to a Modern Jesuit," 23)

In the following passage, Rahner's Ignatius expounds his vision of a solidarity with the Church that includes a critical distancing from what actually occurs within it.

ALLEGIANCE TO THE CHURCH

Now I must also say something about my allegiance to the Church, and about what it means for your time. Everyone expects this, and not unfairly. I could rightly be allowed to be very brief here, considering the objective significances of the realities I am talking about. God, Jesus, following Jesus, and the Church, for all the connections between them, are after all quite different things, and therefore carry different weight. I therefore have not only the right but the obligation, both in time and eternity, to make a real distinction between them as regards their import and significance.

People call me a man of the Church and stress the fact; Marcuse calls me a soldier of the Church.[6] Truly, I am not ashamed of this allegiance to the Church. Once converted, I wanted to serve the Church with my whole life, although even this service was for God and for humanity, not for a self-seeking institution. The Church has infinite dimensions, because it is the community, filled with God's spirit, of people who have faith, who are pilgrims in hope, who are loving God and humanity. But this Church is also — and for me unquestionably so — also a socially constituted Church, particular, shaped by specific history, a Church of institutions, of human words, of identifiable sacraments, of bishops, of the pope of Rome, the hierarchical, Roman Catholic Church. When people call me a man of the Church and when I profess this as a matter of course, then they are referring to the Church precisely in its visible, hard institutional quality, to the institutional Church, as you often say today, with the not particularly pleasant nuance this word has. Yes: I was this man of this Church; that was what I wanted to be, and in it I never seriously found an absolute conflict between my conscience's radical immediacy to God and my mystical experience.

But you would totally misunderstand this allegiance to the Church that I had were you to take it as an egocentric love of power, fanatically setting ideological boundaries and leaving conscience defeated, or as an identification of myself with a "system" that had no reference to anything beyond itself. Given that as we human beings live our lives we are shortsighted and

6. See Ludwig Marcuse, *Soldier of the Church: The Life of Ignatius Loyola*, trans. Christopher Lazare (New York: Simon and Schuster, 1939).

sinful, I certainly do not want to say that back then I did not oc-
casionally pay tribute to this false style of Church allegiance; if
it takes your fancy, go ahead and look honestly and realistically
through my life for this. But what follows is certain: overall my
allegiance to the Church was only one aspect — however indispensable I saw it as being — of my desire "to help souls"; and
this desire attains its goal only to the extent that these "souls"
grow in faith, hope, and love, in immediacy to God.

All love for the institutional Church would be slavery to
idols, complicity in a horrendous self-centered and self-enclosed
system, if it were not inspired and informed — and limited — by
this desire. But this also means (and the history of my mystical
journey bears this out) that love for this Church, however unconditional in a certain sense it may have been, is certainly not
the be-all and end-all of my existence (as you put it today), but
a derived reality, originating in immediacy to God, and depending on this intimacy for its import, its limit, and its nature — a
quite specific nature.

I will say the same thing again in a somewhat different way.
It was as a way of taking part in God's action inclining toward
the particular body God's Son had in history that I loved the
Church: it was in this mystical union of God with the Church —
for all that the two are radically to be distinguished — that the
Church was and remained for me transparent to God, and the
specific place of this ineffable relationship I had to the eternal mystery. Here you have the source of my feeling for the
Church, of my practice of the sacramental life, of my loyalty
to the papacy, of the rootedness in the Church of my mission
to help souls.

If this is the place, this and no other, that this allegiance
to the Church has in the structure of my spiritual life, then
it is still ecclesial to have even a critical relationship with the
institutional Church as it actually is. This kind of critical rela-

tionship on the part of individual Christians is possible because their point of view is not simply absolutely identical with this official Church if you take its visible instititutionality in isolation. For Christians too are always in immediacy to God; they are inspired by grace — for all that this gracious inspiration leaves them where they are in the Church and is also itself proper to the Church as a community of grace — in ways that are not simply mediated by the Church set-up; this inspiration can certainly be a reality from which the institutional Church, in its office-bearers, must learn something if they are not culpably to betray this kind of movement of the Spirit just because they have not first been sanctioned officially by Church authority.

Seen from the Church's side too, this kind of critical relationship to the Church does not cease to be ecclesial. For the Church, even as an institution, remains ultimately open to God's Spirit, subject to the Spirit, on account of God's inclining action to the Church — this Spirit which is always more than institution, law, the letter of the tradition, and so on. Of course, this relationship between Spirit and institution does not, right from the start, just get rid of particular conflicts arising between Christians impelled by the Spirit and the Church's officeholders; such conflicts indeed will always be turning up surprisingly, in new forms, with the result that there are no ready formulae and institutional mechanisms on hand in advance to help us overcome them.

Ultimately it is only in faith that Christians can have the conviction of there not being any necessity until time ends for an absolute conflict between Spirit and institution in the Church. And for themselves, all they can do is humbly hope that God's providence never brings about any situation in their own lives in which they cannot any longer hold together an absolute claim of Church authority and an absolute claim of their conscience as mutually compatible. At any rate, conflicts within the Church itself, particular and limited conflicts, are still ecclesial — and I can say this without having here particular procedures for settling them. Equally, the literal carrying out of a command from above is not the most important imperative involved in allegiance to the Church and of ecclesial obedience, just as I myself, as general of my Society, did not govern through this principle. If this *were* the highest principle, then conflicts in the Church could just never happen. But they do happen; they happen with the saints, and indeed between saints (beginning with the argument between Peter and Paul); and therefore they can legitimately happen.

Even in the Church, there is no principle that says that the convictions and decisions of Christians at large and of office-holders should fit together without friction. The Church is a Church of the Spirit, the Spirit of the infinite God past all grasp. Its blessed unity can be reflected only in this world as broken into many different realities. Between these it is only God's self, and nothing else, that is the ultimate, reconciled unity.

— "Ignatius of Loyola Speaks to a Modern Jesuit," 26–28

"There is no principle that says that the convictions . . . of Christians at large and of officeholders should fit together without friction." In 1973, Rahner wrote a piece of journalism marking the bicentenary of the Jesuits' suppression and at the same time reflecting on what it was to be a Jesuit in the upheaval immediately after Vatican II. From his reflections on Church and culture there emerges a personal, moving statement of his faith and of his sense of vocation. A commitment to a God greater than any human project cannot be identified with any particular belief-system, nor will it necessarily be reciprocated by others in the Church. What matters is the faith that remains patiently committed, whether or not the ruptures are healed in our lifetime.

THE JESUITS AND THE FUTURE

On July 21, 1773, Pope Clement XIV, under pressure from the Bourbon courts, suppressed the Society of Jesus after a good two hundred years of its existence. It was restored forty-one years later, in 1814, by Pius VII, and since then has been carrying on its work. The anniversary this last July provided Jesuits and others an occasion not just for looking back on history, but also for critical reflection on the present state of the Society.

Neither friend nor foe will now dispute that the Society has not been able in the last 160 years to maintain the level of historical significance that it once had in the Catholic Church and therefore in the world at large, even though it still today (despite a not insignificant diminution in the last few years) still has more members than at the time of its suppression. The world, quite simply, has become so much larger and more differentiated, and the "Christian" West no longer has the kind of leadership role that would enable us to expect a religious order of this kind still to be able to occupy, ecclesiastically and culturally, the place that it once did.

If we look at the matter more straightforwardly, the Society of Jesus has in the last few years radically changed its image. Until the Second Vatican Council (more or less) it was thought of as the guardian and defender of strict Church orthodoxy and devotion to the pope as regards faith and morals, as an agent of good order, of unity, of tried and tested tradition, of neo-scholasticism. This old picture may itself be one-sided and too unnuanced (Pius X before World War I suspected the top leadership of the Society of modernism) — but it was what people thought, and in general terms it was not false.

It was not just that the Jesuits saw themselves as true soldiers of the pope (which in fact they still want to be today): it was also that they thought they knew exactly what this fundamental attitude should amount to in terms of practical norms and actions. Today, that is different. The Jesuits are thought of — again, only in general terms — as belonging to the "left," "progressive" wing in the Church. Both in theory and in practice. Rather than list individual instances, Teilhard de Chardin can stand for many people and many things. How can we explain this phenomenon (obviously to the extent that this is possible)? For it is only if we ask this why-question that we can really see the phenomenon for what it is.

You can name three very different reasons that have to be looked at together. First: even the Jesuits are paying their tribute to the "spirit of the age." How could this ever be avoided entirely? After all, you have to pay some element of this tribute if you are ever to have a voice in your own time. And who ever knows just what tribute is justified and what tribute is wrong, what represents the acceptance of a historical necessity (willed by God, as we Christians say), and what is just silly fashion that will all too soon bring itself into disrepute? Those who claim to know too precisely where one kind of tribute stops and the other starts are to be suspected: their "transcendence of the fashions of the age" may really be just blind dependence on an earlier time's conventions.

Second, by virtue of their own spirituality, Jesuits are people who quite deliberately take a very relative view of everything except the one God, the God who is unpredictable and not subject to human manipulation. They are incapable of simply identifying themselves absolutely with a particular time and with its sense of what life is, with its culture and scholarship. Sometimes, this leads to simplistic compromises and accommodations. But the authentic attitude is deeper, genuine, and primordial: God is ever greater (and therefore also, if you like, ever smaller) than culture, scholarship, Church, pope, and anything institutional, and must not be mistaken for any of these. This means that a Jesuit necessarily has a critical attitude to his own past, precisely where this past was a glorious one. And he remains open for everything that is new, precisely because he cannot make an absolute of the new.

Third, the Church is today caught up in a transformation. Probably this has been too long delayed. For people used to think it a special Christian virtue, the salvation of an imperiled world, intransigently to insist on what had always been the case; and therefore this transformation is now coming very suddenly, and with all the typical features and dangers that arise when something in itself necessary has to be "caught up with" too quickly. Yet a transformation of this kind is necessary if the Church does not want to remain the Church of the peasant and petit-bourgeois classes particular to late European modernity, with ever decreasing membership, but instead to become a Church for the kind of society that has a future. This transformation in the Church is difficult because it has begun too late. It involves the danger of betraying the true substance of Christianity. It is painful. It brings the different levels of the Church, which are at different stages in their awareness, into conflict with each other. But it cannot be avoided — indeed it is still not being engaged in with anything like sufficient seriousness. And that such a transformation should extend into the life of a religious order in the Church is something that stands to reason.

If the Society in its life and activity wanted to be as "monolithic" as many, outside it at least, think it should be, it would just be the representative of a stage in the Church's life that is passing and would not be giving any true service to the Church. Obviously it does not want to collude with any false and silly modernisms, but rather to represent and live out the pure essence of Christianity — that is obvious. It is just that it is not so easy to say what this means concretely. Those who make too precise a claim in this regard must be held suspect of what is fundamentally a barren conservatism. In an unknown future (which just is our lot, however unpleasant it is), there is no clear Ordnance Survey map to take out with all the roads already marked on it precisely. If a religious order were to act as though everything was already clear and that all we had to do was advocate it courageously, this would for me be more suspect than my Society in the state in which it currently finds itself — a state that is certainly not easy or clear.

Many will ask the question how a person today can still be a Jesuit, or seek to become one. This question each Jesuit can answer only very "subjectively."

I would like to put it simply, even if it sounds pious. Not because the Society today despite everything has some not insignificant influence in the Church, not because it is still running even today many universities, producing scholars of all kinds, making its mark in the mass media, and so on. Nor even because in many countries it has certainly placed itself on the side of the poor and oppressed much more clearly than it used to do. Rather, because — quite apart from all the pastoral, ministerial, and ecclesiastical work it does, with or without success — there still lives even today (in my experience) in many of its members a desire for unrewarded, silently performed service, for prayer, for entrusting oneself to God's past-all-graspness, for the trustful acceptance of death whatever the form in which it comes, for Jesus the crucified. And when that is there, then it ultimately does not matter what "significance" a group with a spirit has in the history of human culture or of the Church, or whether such a spirit exists just as much, whether expressly or anonymously, in other groups. This spirit exists.

I think of fellow Jesuits whom I myself have known: my friend Alfred Delp, who signed "with chained hands" his final membership of this Society;[7] of the one who, in an Indian

---

7. Alfred Delp (1907–45), arrested by the Nazis in 1944 on account of involvement in resistance discussions, and executed on February 2, 1945. On December 8, 1944, he was visited by Fr. Franz von Tattenbach and was able validly to make his final profession as a Jesuit (which takes place after priestly ordination). His arrest had forestalled a ceremony planned for August 15, 1944. "With chained hands" is a motif running through his powerful prison writings. See Alan C. Mitchell's edition

village that none of the Indian intellectuals allow themselves to look at, is helping the poor devils[8] dig a well there; of the one who is listening for hours on end to the trials and tribulations of people who only look as though they are innocuous and bourgeois; of the one in Barcelona[9] who allowed himself with his students to be beaten up by the police without the satisfaction of being a revolutionary and the kudos that comes from that; of the one who must stand at deathbeds in the hospital every day, and for whom thus this unique event must become daily routine; of the one who is trying to "peddle" the gospel message in prisons, over and over again, with hardly anyone thanking him, appreciated more for cigarettes than for the Word of the gospel; of the one who is trying, laboriously and without "statistical" success, to awaken a spark of faith, hope, and love in just a few people. Even today, it is figures like these and many others, occasions like these when people give themselves over into the mystery of God, that are what counts in the Society, and are acknowledged as such.

It is wrong to sniff out an ideology here that might be offering consolation to help us cope with the Society's historical insignificance today. Even in the Society's glory days of old, death in Tonkin's bamboo cages or getting worn out in the wretchedness of Paraguay's reductions (their sociopolitical significance meant nothing to those working in them back then) was a more desirable life than one in which the Society's luster was being increased. If you can live out the living spirit of Jesus the crucified in this Society, and if this spirit takes priority over

---

in this Modern Spiritual Masters series, and also Mary Frances Coady, *With Bound Hands: A Jesuit in Nazi Germany — The Life and Selected Prison Letters of Alfred Delp* (Chicago: Loyola Press, 2003).

8. The term "poor devils" — which literally translates the original — betrays an unconsciously patronizing attitude and may provoke righteous anger. It would be dishonest, however, to cut it, and its presence here powerfully underscores Rahner's claims about how we never fully integrate our deepest commitments. As he says in extracts later in this chapter, we need patience with ourselves. –PE

9. Spain in 1973 was still under the Franco dictatorship.

everything social and even ecclesiastical (and I think this is the case today too), then the Society's future is for those who are living in it ultimately a secondary matter, and precisely as such a matter of hope.

When the Society was suppressed in 1773, a Jesuit made a rhyme:

> Should it come to death for me,
> Still will I be eternally,
> Thine, Jesu mine, in loving fealty
> With no Pope or Satan hindering me.[10]

Under much ash, there is still burning today in this Society a love for Jesus past all grasp and for his fate. It is out of that love that the Society is serving the Church. Out of that love, it can also be very critical, both of that Church and of itself. Out of that love it can entrust itself to a history that cannot be predicted in advance; out of that love it can accept in consolation its own life, its success and failure, its prestige and its insignificance, and even (if this must be so) its own death as a sharing in the fate of him whose name (certainly a little presumptuously, but also full of poignant hope) it bears.

— "Die Jesuiten und die Zukunft:
Anläßlich eines historischen Datums,"
Frankfurter Allgemeine Zeitung, August 31, 1973

One final piece on the Church, on the possibilities for devotion to Mary and the saints in our own age, illustrates further Rahner's sense of balance. He knows that theologically these devotions make sense. He has heard, too, that there are strong factors in the culture of our time militating against them. Even

---

10. Efforts to trace the original source have been unsuccessful. What Rahner quotes in archaic German does not scan, and may well have originally been in Latin; Rahner's choice of the word "rhyme" shapes this translation.

as in his old age he dictates an answer to an interview question into a tape recorder, one senses a creative mind struggling to see a meaning in what is happening. There is also an impressive recognition that the gift of making the connections in this context can come only from God.

WHAT SCOPE IS THERE FOR A NEW DEVOTION TO MARY AND TO THE SAINTS?

Sometimes one gets the impression that the younger generation is really looking for a really healthy, deep devotion to Mary. Could you give people with this sort of longing some help to find an approach today to a devotion to Mary, and perhaps also to the saints in general? Is this something to be pursued more intensively, or just nostalgia?

If I may be honest, it doesn't seem to me that the movement toward a new and living devotion to Mary is as strong or visible as one could and should hope. Perhaps there is a certain nostalgia around; perhaps there is also a certain habit of trying to say, think, and write something different in theology, which leads people to take up the old theme of Mariology. But I think it's doubtful that there is any revival today of a large-scale, intense devotion to Mary, or that it's coming back, or even that there is any great longing for it. Of course there *ought* to be something like this, but what you can say and wish for in this connection is really very unclear.

A Christian who believes in the historical Jesus Christ will want to develop a theology of salvation history. In this theology of salvation history there will inevitably come — just as is already there in the New Testament — a reference to Abraham, to Moses, and so on. And then you have Mary — something which, for a Christian, is quite normal and comprehensible: Mary, a decisive — or the decisive — supreme image of those who are redeemed, the redeemed who live out the one history of salvation with each other and for each other. Mary is to be seen as the central, decisive figure among the redeemed within salvation history. It's worth thinking about how to keep alive an awareness of this in the Church, as indeed they tried with the chapter on Mary in Vatican II.

Melting into Transcendence

But there is a twofold problem here, clearly evident. First — at least this is how I see it — those people who have been saved and taken up into God's eternal life have, as far as we are concerned, disappeared, so to speak, and become absorbed. We don't seem to be able to get hold of them as distinguishable realities when set within the infinity of God's mysteries. How many people are there still who, when faced with death or when seriously ill, pray to anyone other than God? Certainly God might be asked to steer and direct their lives in accord with the divine will so that they become better: but does anyone in this situation still also call especially on St. Aloysius or St. Ignatius or Fr. Rupert Mayer[11] or anyone else for help (unless pious nuns put them up to it)? Perhaps there are still such people and there's no objection to them. You can only congratulate them. But, if you are honest, you have — I think — to recognize that it is no easy thing today to imagine there are, alongside and within the God who is in free control of our destiny and salvation, also human beings who have some power with regard to our salvation, human beings whom we can distinguish from each other.

---

11. A Jesuit noted for his charitable work in Munich and for his sermons against Nazism. Imprisoned several times and kept under house arrest during World War II, he died in November 1945 and was beatified in 1987. His shrine in central Munich is well frequented.

I once tried to write something about this in an essay on the invocation of the Saints.[12] Is that essay really any good? Does it cope with the problem in anything other than an abstract and speculative fashion? Does it indeed manage to do anything at all that gives anyone anything for their spiritual life? That's a very obscure, difficult question; and I don't want to claim for myself any great merits or successes in this regard. But you can always say: "A person who knows that God is a God of human beings can relatively easily claim theologically that we don't just carry on existing in some vague way, but that this continuing existence 'after death' is obviously something we can attribute, above all, to the saints: in other words they are *living*." We can also say: the nearer someone is to God, the less it is true that that person is absorbed into God and as such becomes nothingness.

Christianity's sense of the human relationship to God is not one that says the more a person grows closer to God, the more that person's own existence vanishes into a puff of smoke. That was also one of the great things that Erich Przywara brought home to us thirty or forty years ago; or as Paul Claudel said, "You don't have to become nothing to get close to God."[13] And you can say all these things and go on this way in connection with the saints. You can, and indeed should, try to make it clearer that the saints in their specific, earthly life history — and people are certainly interested in *that* today — have not ceased to exist when this history did just because they are dead. On the contrary, this specific, true, genuine, unique, unrepeatable, incomparable history has become something that counts eternally in the sight of God. And therefore it belongs really to us, to

---

12. "Why and How Can We Venerate the Saints" (1964), in *Theological Investigations*, 8:3–23.

13. Erich Przywara (1889–1972) was a German Jesuit philosopher and theologian. Paul Claudel (1868–1955) was a noted French Catholic poet, aphorist, and diplomat. It is not clear just which of his sayings Rahner is alluding to here, and the negatives in the German text do not seem quite right.

the Church, the communion of saints. You can, therefore, stress that the saints don't lose what made them historical individuals just because they have finally and definitively entered the realm of God; rather, in a way that cannot be likened to anything we know, they acquire it finally and definitively, and this becomes a blessing for us.

As I've said, all this is well and good; it can and must be stressed. These aren't just theological things that we say; they can in principle become something spontaneously real. But then there comes, I think, the second difficulty on top of this. This difficulty will need to be overcome if we are ever going to be able to talk of a living devotion to the saints, as it was in the old days.

Lived Love

When I talk about what Napoleon was like as an individual, historically and psychologically; when I study that; or when I get stuck into the life of Goethe — all this can be interesting, and such people can also become significant as models for me to a certain extent. But a personal relationship to a specific, unique, and still living person — you don't get that in this way. If I were to use an example to bring out where, in my opinion, the problem lies, the example would be this: Once upon a time, when kings still sought to marry off their daughters to other noble people and looked around for them, they used to tell these daughters about Prince so-and-so: how decent and rich he was, what a powerful lord he was. And then spontaneously this princess got an abstract picture of her prospective bridegroom — perhaps it was a correct one, but it somehow stayed in general terms. But if I really love someone, then that has to be something different from what I've just been saying about this poor princess. Then there arises a quite personal, unique relationship to a quite specific other person, a relationship that is unmistakable, unique: it's a relationship of personal, life-changing, living love, coming from within.

Genuine devotion to the saints — it seems to me — occurs or would occur only when there is this kind of knowledge between yourself and a saint (of course Mary especially): specific, unique, living, going beyond abstract theories of a historical, theological, or metaphysical kind. But then you need to have a situation in which, so to speak, a spark leaps out, when a unique love arises. Then you've got — I'd like to say — what people call a grace. I can't just produce at will a personal relationship to Mary, for example — whatever theology and its elaborations might say. And the big Mariologies we used to have could be so wonderful in those days because they didn't, deep down, need to produce this immediate, genuine, experienced love; they were rather a secondary outgrowth of this kind of personal love.

Desirable but Not Possible

But then of course the problem arises: What are Christians of today supposed to do? They can to some extent recognize — just theoretically and abstractly — that in a lived Christianity, developed in a fully catholic fashion, a relationship to the saints must be there and makes sense. I don't say all the saints; but the point applies, of course, in a special way to Mary because of her special place in salvation history. And then, if they have got that point, all they can do is wait for the moment of grace, and perhaps *pray for* this sort of moment that will bring about this kind of relationship in them.

After all, something like this happens with Christ — this is not to deny Christology or to be reductive. If I just study Christology, then I'm studying a complicated system of theoretically correct statements — but in the end they are just theoretical.

And if I love Jesus Christ, if the grace has been given me really to love this specific Jesus, just as he was back then and just as he has finally and definitively become before God with the history he had back then, in this personal way — then I'm no longer just a Christian in theory, but, in a good sense, one who is part and parcel of the very identity of Christianity, a Jesus-freak, who loves Jesus.[14] And then in this way I can be his disciple, in a way that you can't get out of purely theoretical reflections and theological constructions.

Something like this, *mutatis mutandis,* happens regarding the saints too. Whether anyone manages it is another question. You shouldn't demand anything like this, or want to force it violently. But you can see that there is here a dimension of Christian living that perhaps you haven't fully appropriated for yourself. And you can pray for the gift, and prepare yourself for it, of an inward understanding of this personal relationship to a particular saint, and especially to Mary.

"Postmodern" critics of Rahner, both within and beyond Catholicism, have failed to see how much he shares their concern. He may still believe, literally and without complication, in an all-knowing God, but he is well aware that human knowing is always partial, always shaped by its own situation, inevitably pluralist. This kind of "educated ignorance," of realistic acceptance that we have to live our lives largely without understanding everything we might wish to understand, was a virtue he came to value more and more in his old age. Two essays, one on an "unknown virtue," and one on patience, develop the theme outside directly ecclesiastical settings.

---

14. The German here plays on a preoccupation of Rahner's later years: the need to distinguish Christianity from what he called "Jesuanity (*Jesuanismus*)," a style of enthusiastic, Jesus-centered piety that rejects or ignores any of the metaphysical issues arising from a claim that Jesus of Nazareth is in some sense God.

PLEA FOR AN UNNAMED VIRTUE

All over the world, people have explicitly seen and named virtues, that is, ethically good ways of behaving. Perhaps they were only wanting to be able to make a demand on others. But still: expressly giving things names like this, and making distinctions is both inevitable and useful. You see more clearly what you have to do; you can check more easily whether you are really fulfilling the ethical demands placed on you by the person you are and the life you are leading. Moral theologians and philosophers have developed whole systems of virtues, with lots of classifications and relationships of mutual dependence, so that there are no empty gaps in the map of moral obligation.

Perhaps moral philosophy and theology is less bothered these days with counting out the virtues systematically in this way — this is because it is concerned with questions that come prior to any such description and classification of the particular ways in which we may behave. Perhaps people also have the sense that this kind of old-fashioned, systematic catalogue of virtues isn't all that useful for real life. But human beings and Christians cannot just act; they have to know how and why they are acting amid the unmanageable diversity of life and its tasks. And in the field of ethical freedom, reflection is both legitimate and necessary. So the question about virtues will always have to be asked, repeatedly — however we approach it, and whatever terminology we use to deal with such issues.

Are there virtues that have remained without a name? Virtues that — let us hope — may have been practiced in real life, but that have not been expressly thought through in the reflections of moral philosophy and theology. All human tasks and ways of behaving hang together, and therefore it is of course unlikely that a particular form of moral behavior — albeit little reflected on — cannot in any way be lumped in with a virtue that is already known and expressly named, unlikely therefore that it is has remained completely nameless. But it is nevertheless possible that theoretical reflection about the ethical as a whole does not get hold of each and every individual element with equal clarity. And so this or that ethical way of behavior does in the end remain nameless, vanishing a little too much as we use a general, abstract concept. That something like this is imaginable needs no further argument — it can be shown from the sheer fact that the moral classifications and terminologies of particular times, cultures, and ways of life have been, and still are, very different: you can hardly get them to overlap. Every style of life that has arisen historically involuntarily and inevitably overlooks one virtue or another, a virtue that another style of life recognizes and cultivates. And this indubitable fact cannot be explained simply by how the conditions under which human beings live — independently of morality and before you talk of morality — are different, and therefore require ethically different behavior.

An Anonymous Virtue

A priori, then, we expect that there must be virtues that have remained anonymous. Can we document this with an actual example? As was said, if you try to do something like this, you always have to reckon with the objection that what you are talking about has been known and named for ages: it's called this or that. But this doesn't *have* to disturb us: we say at the outset that we are just seeing more clearly what's being referred to, and delimiting it from other, more general realities into which previously it vanished. The question that remains consists of course in the question of whether or not you can also suggest a short new name that can be understood. But even if you can't suggest a short and clear baptismal name for what you are referring to and what you have found, the task we have set ourselves still remains sensible and feasible. In this case you

just use a lot of words to draw attention to a particular ethical style of behavior and leave it to others to find a single,
comprehensible word for it.

We begin from a discrepancy that occurs at least frequently,
or even most of the time: that between how the rational and
reflective reasons for a moral attitude are problematic and insecure, on the one hand, and how a decision made in freedom
is absolute. We always — or at least most of the time — have
good reasons for a moral decision, let us hope. But these are
rarely simply beyond the possibility of doubt. Rather, in most
cases there are good reasons and arguments for an opposite decision. Yet what we do in freedom, as such, points only in one
direction: it is absolute and quite literally irreversible. The decision cannot be made with a sense of "on the one hand and
on the other," with the reservations that are part and parcel
of rational reflection. All the traditional "moral systems"[15] in
Catholic moral theology are based on this gulf between a theory that is not definite and a practice that must be definite: they
try to give principles about how a person can, in practice, come
to terms with this conflict. These principles do not interest us
here any further. What is important here is what all these systems are based on: the fact that very often the ethical reflection
that comes before the act itself cannot deliver the definiteness
and unquestionable sureness with which, willy-nilly, one is then
acting in the action itself.

Skeptical Relativism

In this situation, within which we human beings find ourselves
thousands of times, we can initially think of two reactions (false
ones). We can be *skeptical* and *relativist,* and write off the significance of the ethical reflection that happens before the action,

---

15. A technical term from an older theology denoting various approaches to
conflict of duties.

on the ground that, seeing that it cannot deliver the absolute definiteness that inevitably marks the action, nothing depends on it. Precisely on questions of religion or worldview, this relativistic attitude is very widespread. We are aware of how any particular justification of a decision about a world view, developed by a rational fundamental theology, will have problems, and we conclude that this reflection is useless and superfluous and feel justified in making the decision arbitrarily, at whim: "It's a matter of where we were born," and so on. Our indecision becomes hardened into a theory, and we lose the desire to commit ourselves. And we think this way we can avoid a decision — even though in reality this is not the case, since even this kind of refusal to make a decision is still a decision of the kind in question, and quite certainly not the best decision.

Ideological Fanaticism

Alternatively, we refuse to see how the ethical reflection that precedes a decision will have problems. We deny the validity, for ourselves and for others, of these problems. We explain that the rational and conscious argument for our own decision is in every respect absolutely illuminating: there are no serious arguments at all against it that haven't long ago and quite definitely been refuted for any honest and sensible person. This kind of *ideological fanaticism* was, until very recently, all too often common among Christians in the squabbles between the different Churches. And again, when it came to giving arguments in apologetics or in fundamental theology for worldviews, people on both sides acted all too often as if everything was clear in the justification of their own standpoint, and only ignorance or bad will was capable of not understanding this. Even the language of the First Vatican Council (DS 3009)[16] still rather naively

---

16. This reference in Rahner's text points to chapter 3 of Vatican I's decree, *Dei filius,* in particular to a paragraph describing how "exterior proofs" of God's

starts from the supposition that the true religion must include irrefutable justifications in the sphere of fundamental theology, which in fact any well-educated and well-disposed human being should be able to understand without further ado. Catholic fundamental theology was not always and everywhere free from the mistake of supposing that the certainty of the arguments in fundamental theology must more or less match the absoluteness of the assent of faith. But in all fields (not just the religious one), this kind of attitude — which wants to transfer the unavoidable once-and-for-allness of a free decision back onto the weighing up of the objective and moral justification for it — is precisely the real nature of ideological fanaticism.

Skeptical relativism that thinks it can dispense itself from making a decision, and ideological fanaticism that wants to derive the absolute nature of a decision in freedom from an absoluteness in rational reflection of a kind that just does not exist — these are the two false conclusions that people can very easily draw from the irresoluble difference that exists between a reflection that will always involve problems and a decision that will always be once and for all, the difference between theory and practice.

Between the Extremes

Between these two extremes, there is a middle ground. It is a virtue, and this virtue seems to me not to have a name. In this middle ground, one takes seriously prior reflection about whether a decision is legitimate, and yet one does not demand more from this reflection than it can give: the problems with it are honestly admitted. Despite this, the problems do not stop us having the courage to make calm, courageous decisions. They

---

revelation — "divine facts, especially miracles and prophecies" — corroborate the commitments of faith.

reflect what human beings are, rightly understood: they are neither Gods of absolute, comprehensive security and clarity; nor are they beings of empty whim, for which everything is equally true and equally false. They have contours that are to be respected, even though these do not have the brilliance of the divine and the self-evident.

It is difficult to hold on to this middle ground. For when it comes to applying this in practice, once again there is no simple and obvious and indisputable principle that can justify it. It belongs with that wisdom that knows how to make the best of things, a wisdom that rational acuteness alone cannot deliver. In the end it does not matter whether or not you want to join Thomas Aquinas and call it an intellectual or a moral virtue. It is the virtue that really takes theoretical rationality seriously, and yet does not simply reduce practice to something secondary to theory, derivative from it, but rather acknowledges that freedom in the end stands on its own, and cannot be just deduced. It is the virtue of active respect for how theory and practice, knowledge and freedom, are at the same time mutually related and mutually independent. It is the virtue of both the union and the difference between these two realities, not sacrificing either in the interests of the other.

It seems to me that this kind of behavior exists, and therefore this kind of human virtue. But what are we meant to call it? That is difficult to say. If you were to call it the courage to make decisions in a way that is sensible, and yet is not simply the product of rationality, then you would have chosen a name that is too general and vague, because it would of course embrace more than has been referred to here. So it seems that this virtue, which is not unimportant, has no short, generally comprehensible name. Perhaps the ultimate reason for this is that the relationship between theory and practice is still an obscure problem in philosophy. You can lump the virtue we are trying to find here in with prudence, or perhaps with wisdom. But it is "lumping in," of the kind that makes something specific get lost in something general. Whether this virtue has a well-known name or not is in the end not so important. But this virtue should be exercised, especially today, when you can easily have the impression that the majority of people are divided between the weary relativists and the stubborn fanatics.

ON INTELLECTUAL PATIENCE WITH ONESELF

Precisely when it comes to the simplest things, which a wise person does spontaneously, people can only talk in an awkward and boring way. Among these simple things, in my opinion, is patience with oneself.

That people in general must be patient with themselves seems to me something obvious — but it is one of the obvious things that people manage only rather badly. There may be people who think they do not need to be patient with themselves, because they are completely satisfied with themselves and with what they do — and I hope we will not envy the happy state of these integrated souls. But in truth we are probably people — if we are honest with ourselves — who have not yet come to terms with ourselves. And nor can we just summon up the state of perfect satisfaction with ourselves just by commanding it or by some sort of psychological gimmick or the like. So, since we are not fully satisfied with ourselves, and since this peace is not within our own power, we need to have patience with ourselves.

The person in us, the person we really are, finds confrontation with the person we want to be painful. (Here we are leaving aside the questions about whether we could still be human beings, still in becoming and having a future before ourselves, if this difference was not there; about whether this peace with ourselves would not be death; and about how we could imagine this peace in such a way that we could still strive for it in the form of eternal life and eternal peace.)[17]

Be all that as it may, we are now living on the way; we are living between a past and a future that are both in their different ways out of our control. We never have it all together — all that inevitably shapes our lives. We are always shaped by our history, manipulated by our society, biologically under threat — and we know it. We can try to repress our knowledge of this situation; we can try just to sit with the brute fact that we cannot change; we can abuse what truly are the pleasant things in life to kill the pain of the mysterious dissatisfaction in our life; when this hidden dissatisfaction presses forward, we can interpret it as psychological depression, which one either has just to live with or else fight with every possible kind of psychiatric medication.

But if we have the courage to let this dissatisfaction actually confront us, if one gives it its due and accepts it, without just interpreting it as the stuff that fosters heroes, or else despairing on its account — then we are having patience with ourselves. One has come to accept that one has not yet found pure self-acceptance. There will be lots of people who think they have this patience, and that it is the easiest thing in the world. But if such people were to look more closely within themselves, they would notice that they are not really accepting the pain of their own unredeemed restlessness in patience, without hating it. Rather, they are just running away into everyday triviality and claiming in this way to be realistic and down to earth. Or else what dominates them is an unacknowledged despair, or a despairing resignation: in the end they think that there is no reason for them to live. As they look at how their whole being is called into question, they are not being patient: they are

---

17. A seminal early essay of Rahner's, "The Theological Concept of Concupiscentia" (1939), *Theological Investigations*, 1:347–82 suggested that the human process of becoming was not necessarily an effect of the Fall from perfection but was intrinsic to our identity under God.

studiedly trying to look the other way and get hold of some substitute for patience that can also allow them — or so they think — to live.

Patience and Composure

But patient persons really suffer their restlessness and accept it. They let their pain mean something. Really patient persons also accept, with some suffering, that they do not know for sure if they are *really* accepting this restlessness with patience, or else just giving in to it with a triviality that only looks like patience. Patient persons are patient with their own impatience; and so they can, serenely and almost cheerfully, make do without any ultimate self-acceptance. They do not know where they get it from — this composure in which they can let themselves be themselves. They hope they have got it. Indeed even allow themselves, in cheerful hope, to allow themselves the painkillers used by the impatient — for they too are allowed to use them precisely because they don't regard them as having any ultimate effect. The patient person is a person of composure, and therefore a free person. [...]

Perhaps you have already become impatient and think this impatience is justified. Perhaps it is, if it is about my talking about patience. But it is not justified if it is directed against the reality itself that my stammering words are trying to point to: how patience holds together what is divided, the holding together — called "patience" — that I am imagining is there in you.

The Present Mental Climate: Boundless Knowledge

If now we are to go on to talk about intellectual patience — or, better, about the patience with the limitations and unpredictability of our knowledge, we must first talk about the mental climate in which we, inescapably, find ourselves, in a way different from previous times. There has never been a time when humanity knew so much as it does now. Human beings today do not just have some vague idea about how to eke out and defend their biological lives; they are no longer respecting the memory of the past in myth, saga, and perhaps a little history; they are no longer just laboriously and perhaps with lots of mistakes doing a little metaphysics; they are not just practicing religion and stammering in many languages about the divine.

Today human beings do serious study. They research the natural world systematically. In psychology and psychoanalysis they can see for themselves how they tick. More recently, they have conquered whole new fields of knowledge, like the social sciences. They develop a theory of how these various studies of theirs relate and explore once again the history of them all. Out of their daily experiences and insights, they build themselves a systematic body of knowledge. They develop methods of data processing and systems for storing their knowledge. This whole enterprise of formal knowledge involves people of every nation and affects how they live their lives. They are involved in incessant interaction. The number of books that gets printed is accelerating with dizzying speed: libraries get bigger and bigger; new ways of storing knowledge are invented. The progress of knowledge is no longer a matter left to chance, to unpredictable ideas and inspirations, but rather something foreseen systematically in advance — even if, within this system, new unpredictabilities arise, even if no one can plan how all these disciplines and the ways they take will fit together.

But if "we" today know immeasurably more than "we" did, then you fall at once into a terrible problem when you ask who this "we" is who knows so much and is acquiring more and more knowledge at this kind of speed. It's not me; no individual persons these days can embody this "us" who knows such an enormous amount. We have had to stop trying to be universally competent and knowledgeable. The cleverest persons are condemned to be idiots beyond their own specialization[18] and remain that way. Of course you can still even today strive for the most rounded possible education and put the *Encyclopaedia Britannica* or the like on your bookshelf (where there will always be only a pathetically small quantity of books); you can hang around reference libraries; you can let other people tell you in so-called interdisciplinary dialogue what they know and can tell you — but in the end you come away with the impression that you don't after all understand what the representative of another field of knowledge is saying. Of course to some extent you can enjoy the fruits of others' knowledge by switching on the radio or by using a computer that you couldn't build for yourself; and you can learn the tricks you need in order to act as though you can join in any conversation without betraying your ignorance. But all this in the end is no use whatever.

If you are making comparisons about the quantity of knowledge in principle available at a particular time, individuals today are becoming increasingly more stupid. In earlier times "we" knew *relatively* little; but of that little it was possible for an individual to know the lot. Today "we" know a great deal; but each individual knows only a tiny bit of it. You can, admittedly, store up this huge mass of knowledge in libraries and computers and no doubt also invent ways and means for individuals too to call up, quickly and conveniently, from this mass of knowledge just what they need here and now, or just what has whetted their curiosity. But this can work only if the individuals are still able to recognize that something might be useful or interesting for them here and now, something that they don't yet know — and this proviso is by no means to be taken for

---

18. *Fachidiot:* the *idiot* also suggests a lack of proportion. The word has its roots in a Germanic approach to scholarship.

granted any more. And, in itself, all this knowledge stored up in books and computers is actually only the material deposit of what is *really* knowledge. It becomes real knowledge only if it is brought into the consciousness of real human beings — if you tried to put a human library on Mars, it would cease to be human. The difference between now and earlier times is that this knowledge in material form can't as a whole be transferred back to the individual consciousness as such. And so the point still holds: the individual as such — and only in the individual can real knowledge exist — is becoming ever more stupid. [...]

Patience as a Way to God

I'd like now to attempt, hesitantly, to name some implications of this patience with our situation that is demanded of us, implications which might illustrate somewhat further what is actually meant by this intellectual virtue of patience, this unknown virtue.

First, this patience is, after all, related to the true *docta ignorantia* (educated ignorance) about which philosophers speak from a distance and which the mystics of East and West try to attain. If we realize that around the pathetic little island of our knowledge there spreads out an unending sea of the mystery without a name, and if we can use the ideas we've just been talking about to become even clearer about this insight, then perhaps this twofold insight — the two bits working together — might after all suggest to us, awaken in us, the enormous courage that those saints and mystics had who spoke of being absorbed in God. For they no longer experience this sea bounding the "tiny island of their knowledge" as a frontier constricting them. They dare to move themselves out onto this sea; they have no fear that its silent immensity would swallow them up; they entrust themselves to this known Unknown as to the mystery that enfolds them in blessedness. They venture onto and into the Void of their awareness. In the "nothing" as far as individual items of knowledge go — these have all passed away — they experience and recognize the real, embracing Truth in a way that is no longer to be broken up into a number of individual statements.

We cannot touch further here on this ineffable mystery that transforms the pain of ignorance, the pain of our stupidity, into the blessedness of the light that seems like a Dark Night to our everyday consciousness. We also don't need to issue long warnings against the danger that at least the Christian sees — the Christian *knows* that the patient endurance of our earthly complexity and contradiction is ultimately the same as the only way, the way that leads through a real death with Jesus the crucified one into the blessed past-all-graspness of the true God; they *know* that true mystics must always be ready to abandon their high contemplation, their mystical silence, in order to give bread to the hungry; they *know* that the great feast of blessed union with the mystery past all grasp can ultimately only be the fruit of the bitter weeks of daily drudge and its duties. The precise point to be noted here is simply the suggestion that the patience this talk is meant to be extolling can also be the gate leading into that *docta ignorantia* that brings human knowledge, with all its scattered details, into the Light that we Christians — even today — have no inhibition about calling God.

Patience and Tolerance

But this patience with our cognitive situation has other still further implications. Let's start with tolerance. Of course people say that we human beings should be tolerant with each other. But truth marks itself off quite remorselessly, intolerantly, from error — at least initially, that is a principle that can and must be held. Even in this context, no houseroom should be made for complacent relativism. There is also nothing to be said against

the point that specific decisions of rightly exercised freedom are
inevitably, whether we like it or not, tied up with a certain harsh
intolerance toward other people who want to decide differently.
Things in the world cannot always and in every case be decided
with a compromise that suits everyone.

Nevertheless, if what we have been saying about the basis of
intellectual patience is right, you can see that the truth that is
our truth, not the truth of God, involves intrinsically and of its
very nature a dimension of tolerance. For what we have been
saying implies that these very sentences and concepts of ours —
however right and true they may be and however much they
do not acknowledge the opposite as equally true — nevertheless involve intrinsically a reference to what is unknown. And
this "unknown" reality, were it to be known and taken into
account, would also let these sentences and concepts that refer beyond themselves appear in another light. The Unknown
would require us to understand these sentences, with their truth
that borders onto the Unknown, more cautiously. It would enable us to see why our limited sentences, uttered at a particular
point in history, should — even when they remain true — ex-
clude as wrong much less of what other people try to express as
truth. There was a tag in scholastic philosophy — "if you don't
mention things you're not thereby lying — *abstrahentium non
est mendacium.*"[19] That statement is true, but it is also a dan-
gerous one, one that can always be intolerantly misused by the
zealots of their own convictions. It is not just in God's heaven
that there are many mansions, but also in the house of the one
all-embracing Truth.

Those who feel the pain of their own stupidity and endure it
in patience can — even when it comes to talking about religion
and worldviews — be more tolerant, more genuinely tolerant

---

19. Quoted, for example, in Thomas Aquinas, *Summa theologiae*, 1.7.3, who in
turn cites Aristotle's *Physics*, book 2 (193b 35).

than those who look on tolerance only as a convenient tool for people who have to live with each other even when their opinions are different. Perhaps someone has the impression that you can only with difficulty reconcile the proper absoluteness of truth with the tolerance that we have been trying just now to show as being an intrinsic property of *our* truth. But before people try the various possible strategies for resolving this apparent contradiction — strategies we certainly need — I would say that we just have to concede that there is, for the moment, a certain unreconciledness between an inexorable commitment to truth and tolerance, and that we just have to put up with this, in the very patience we have been talking about. It can by all means be the case that this reconciliation between tolerance and inexorable conviction is just as much something we just have to deal with, over and over again, as are the thousands of other cases in which we have to hold on to two truths and convictions without our being able to see clearly how they are in themselves compatible, despite their looking contradictory. Those who really exhibit patience with themselves will also be tolerant with their neighbor and not behave as if they themselves were absolute truth in person. [...]

Patience as Virtue

In the old days people were convinced that knowledge, in its own right, was not just a matter of developing technical skills; in this very sphere of knowledge there were states of mind that could be described in moral terms, in other words virtues — however paradoxical this sort of statement may seem at first sight. Our own time is largely blind and can see in knowledge only a capacity that is ultimately value-neutral and therefore in some way without responsibility — not a virtue. Generally, therefore, it notices only too late the disasters that this approach to knowledge that is blind to values can bring about. But we can't deal further with all that here.

I am going to stop talking about the patience that we must have today when confronted with how our knowledge is limited. I hope I have not with all this overtaxed *your* patience. It seems to me that precisely the progress in all dimensions of knowledge that we are experiencing today makes individuals feel more and more that they don't know much and can't overcome the inadequacy in their knowledge. They feel denied the ecstatic happiness that came in earlier ages when new knowledge was acquired; at the same time, they don't feel entitled to commit intellectual suicide. And so they feel that, as if in a time of winter, they must have patience with themselves.

The same qualities of gentle acceptance that some problems cannot be solved comes through our second extract from Mein Problem, *in which Rahner tries to answer a sensitive and generous young man obviously shaken by what he has experienced when visiting an old people's home.*

THANKING GOD
WHEN THERE'S SO MUCH PAIN?

Dear Fr. Rahner:

I'm especially proud to have the chance of writing to you because just in the last few months (since I've been involved a bit with what's going on in Church and been reading some theological stuff) I've been hearing and reading a lot about you, and thus know how important you are for the Church and for believers. So obviously I was really happy about your visit and the Mass you did with us — and I have a (for me) special bond with you because I am the young person to whom you gave the opera ticket. Thank you very much indeed!

Our youth club has got a kind of "voluntary service group" in which I've got fully involved. What I do there is basically quite simple. I don't need to do anything else except care for an old person who is on their own in a home, for example, by visiting that person once a week.

I found this meeting with old people a great challenge, because up till now I've hardly ever had anything to do with old people (I see my grandparents at most three times a year because they live really far away).

I've been churned up by this meeting the whole year and quite bothered with it: very often it made me think and (even more often) ask questions: it's opened my eyes. The first time I went there with a lot of idealism — I wanted to give these people a change, someone to talk to, a bit of energy and happiness. But this idealism soon got sat on: the whole climate and atmosphere there was terribly depressing. Not one of them could care less. Even when I tried to make some-one laugh, I just got looked at blankly. The whole home is just an enormous dumping ground: you're just a number among the four thousand others they've got there.

For a year I've been visiting a certain Mrs. M. She's nearly eighty; she's been in the home for six years and spends almost the whole time in bed because her legs are paralyzed. That said, in her own way she's still one of the fittest people in her ward. At the start I was always disappointed at how little my visit seemed to do for her. Her reaction was always something between suspicious and indifferent. But as I kept the contact going and our relationship be-came deeper, something else struck me: that she (and probably most of the others too) was so embittered at what was going on there and also because of her age and especially because of her incredi-bly great personal suffering. This embitteredness was also why they had so many rows with each other — often childish ones. And also why patients who had been in beds next to each other hardly ever spoke to each other any more because they were suspicious. One result of this embitteredness was that they often looked so dreadfully couldn't-care-less to outsiders.

The same evening I go on to a prayer group. We sing lots of nice songs about God's closeness and God's love — and lots of people also give thanks for something or other that has happened during the day. But I find thanks very difficult. Of course I can give thanks for my life too — I'm doing really well. But how can I really be grateful when I'm always inevitably thinking about the question that this old lady put to me (and she's got a lot of faith): "Why have I got to suffer all this, when I've really tried my whole life long to live in the way God wants me to? Why doesn't God let me die — I want an end to this whole life."

Once all this was particularly heavy. Between the old people's home and the prayer group I looked quickly at the news on TV: once again an earthquake had led to a huge loss of life. After that I just couldn't join in the singing: all this stuff seemed of course very nice, just like a dream, but in the end just the image of our own wishes, a pious pretend world.

Fr. Rahner, I'd like to ask you to help me sort out this conflict.

Best wishes

Alex

Dear Alex:

First of all, I find it really good that you go and visit this old people's home and find out about what human life can sink to while most people your age protect themselves from that. You won't always be able to work in an old person's home like this, but you are now doing something that is really Christian and are learning a great deal from it that will help you live an adult Christian life.

Of course I can't write about all the problems of these homes where so many old people are crammed in. But precisely when there are things like this that shouldn't happen, and when you realize that there's nothing you can do to change them, then you need to do some thinking and sort out how we as Christians can come to terms with this kind of thing in life that we can't understand — things that are wrong, and can't be just got rid of. But I don't want to write about that now. If you think about Christ on the cross, then you've got the sharpest case of this basic problem there is in life, and also the real solution: it's realistic and honest, and yet it also points us to a happy outcome.

You're coming into contact with lots of old people in this home — they are just old, and it may not be their fault they've become embittered. And — to put it bluntly — some of them are senile. Always remember that this kind of suffering and bitterness is certainly awful — but nevertheless, when they're in a state where personal guilt isn't an issue for them anymore (and you don't need to be frightened of claiming that), none of this bothers God: it will get sorted out in eternal life a lot more easily than what really is a matter of guilt and sin, and was done almost automatically when they were healthy. The ultimate problems are, after all, those of sin committed freely before God — and therefore also the suffering and unhappiness that comes *from that.*

Christians too have a hard time understanding this and taking it seriously, but that's the way it is. But then you ask me how God could allow so much suffering of the kind you also experience so close at hand in this old people's home. I once wrote an essay called "Why Can God Let Us Suffer?" This is a short letter, and I hope I can just point you to that piece, which you should be able to get hold of in your parish.[20] But even in that essay, I'm just answering your question — and the old lady's question — by saying that I don't *have* an answer. There are some half-answers that are all right as far as they go, but

20. Translated as "Why Does God Allow Us to Suffer" (1979), in *Theological Investigations,* 19:194–208. One wonders how many parishes, even Jesuit ones, in the English-speaking world have a complete set of Rahner's *Theological Investigations.*

the whole question is unanswerable. We are within the mystery past all grasp, which God is: there the answer is hidden from us. And so, if we accept this suffering in hope, it's only the particular way in which we accept God's own self, God's own eternal past-all-graspness.

I don't know if you can perhaps begin to understand this at sixteen — but human beings are in fact incapable of being wholly satisfied with what they can grasp and see their way round, however fine and beautiful this might be. And if we try to reach beyond this, we inevitably come up against the mystery of God. And then the question is whether we can summon up the rare courage of a love that is convinced of how love for a God whom we can no longer grasp is the true and in the end the only real happiness for humanity. And then they need to bring this courage precisely to face the suffering there is in the world — obviously drawing on a power that comes only from God.

If you recognize that these old, troubled, confined people in the home can't manage anything like this anymore — what for you with the idealism of youth doesn't seem so difficult — then remember too that these protests, complaints, rebellions, that seem to be present in these people at the end of their lives are no longer really personal actions for which these people will have to answer before God.

If someone is stabbed, for example, with a red-hot poker, then even the holiest individuals are just going to cry out and be in a terrible state. They can't think of God any more at that point: they're just devoured by their dreadful pain. These people worked out their love for God at earlier stages of their lives, at a time when they were free and able to take charge of themselves, and at that point given themselves over to the mystery of God. And often it'll be a bit like this with these old people, too. They can't, perhaps, actually live out a personal relationship with God any more, but we can trust that they once did do this, and that this — what was properly theirs — has been accepted by God. If old persons still hang on to their sanity and their freedom to work out a personal relationship with God right until they die — this can also happen and it's by no means rare — if they (as I know from one of the people in my community) can pray, "In the name of the Father and of the Son and of the Holy Spirit," and then die — then that's wonderful and it's a grace of God. But if you find angry and embittered old people in the home who can't manage this any more — well then, it's still a tough experience that it's hard to stomach, like all experiences of the suffering in the world that doesn't make sense. But it's also an experience that doesn't need to shake you out of your basic Christian optimism. Such people have long ago been caught up in a love of God that is silent.

Every good wish to you, and for what you do in the old people's home and in the parish.

Yours

Karl Rahner

— *Is Christian Life Possible Today?* 29–35

Rahner's attempts to theologize about old age here remind us of the final unknown: death. The theme of death had marked Rahner's writing from the beginning — On the Theology of Death *is one of his most significant shorter books. Rahner's final public lecture of any substance took place in Freiburg, his birthplace, in February 1984, marking his eightieth birthday. He looked back on eighty years as a theologian, speaking of various things he had learned from his theological experience. He spoke of the principle of analogy; of grace as God's gift of self; of the Ignatian tradition; of the relationship between theology and other fields of knowledge as they grow exponentially. He concludes with a peroration about death and the afterlife. It centers on a simple question — "but how, but how?" — answered by a magnificent, apophatic sentence that is 280 words long in this translation and 235 in the German.*

THAT WHICH IS TO COME

I want to talk about one more thing I've realized from experience, an insight that cuts right across everything I have said so far, and therefore cannot be counted in as one insight among others: the sense of awaiting "that which is to come." If as Christians we believe in the eternal life as something we are meant to share in, there is nothing particularly strange about the expectation of what is yet to come. Normally people talk with a certain unctuous sentimentality about hope in eternal life; far be it from me to criticize anything like this when it is honestly meant. But speaking for myself, it comes across as strange when I hear people talk like this. It seems to me that the models and schemes people use to try and explain eternal life in general don't fit the radical rupture that nevertheless comes with death. People think to themselves about an eternal life that is generally described — and this is already strange — as "on the other side" and "after" death; these thoughts are dressed up too much with realities that are familiar to us here: continuing to live on; meeting with those who were close to us here; friends; happiness; banquets; joy and all that kind of thing. These things are presented as never ceasing, as carrying on. I'm worried that the radical past-all-graspness of what "eternal life" really refers to is being rendered innocuous, and that what we call the immediate vision of God in this eternal life is being leveled down to one among others of the pleasant occupations that fill this life. The ineffable outrageousness of the absolute Godhead in person falling stark naked into our narrow creaturehood is not being perceived authentically. I confess that it seems to me an agonizing task for today's theologian — one that hasn't been managed —

to discover a better imaginative model for this eternal life that prevents these devaluings from the outset. But how? But how?

When the angels of death have swept all the worthless rubbish that we call our history out of the rooms of our consciousnesses (though of course the true reality of our actions in freedom will remain); when all the stars of our ideals, with which we ourselves in our own presumption have draped the heaven of our own lived lives, have burned out and are now extinguished; when death has built a monstrous, silent void, and we have silently accepted this in faith and hope as our true identity; when then our life so far, however long it has been, appears only as a single, short explosion of our freedom that previously presented itself to us stretched out in slow motion, an explosion in which question has become answer, possibility reality, time eternity, and freedom offered freedom accomplished; when then we are shown in the monstrous shock of a joy beyond saying that this monstrous, silent void, which we experience as death, is in truth filled with the originating mystery that we call God, with God's light and with God's love that receives all things and gives all things; and when then out of this pathless mystery the face of Jesus, the blessed one, appears to us and this specific reality is the *divine surpassing* of all that we truly assume regarding the past-all-graspness of the pathless God — then, then I don't want actually to describe anything like this, but nevertheless, I do want to stammer out some hint of how a person can for the moment expect what is to come: by experiencing the very submergence that is death as already the rising of what is coming. Eighty years is a long time. But for all of us, the lifetime assigned to us is the short moment in which what is meant to be comes to be.

— "Experiences of a Catholic Theologian," 14–15

After the applause, Rahner stood up and offered his thanks. A collection had been made at the gathering for a priest in Africa who had written to Rahner out of the blue asking for financial help toward a motorcycle. In his appeal, Rahner had said:

> *If you do this, you will make me very happy. For of course my sense is that all our theological talk — clever, profound, magnificent, striking, moving people to tears — is still not as important as when we gave a poor person a bowl of soup (as I think Meister Eckhart said).*

Rahner's final words were unscripted, and the video recorder did not pick them up fully. He thanked people for their gifts and then ended.

> *I thank you warmly, and I ask you — speaking as an ordinary Christian who knows what really matters — to make perhaps just a small prayer in God's presence that His love and His mercy may finally be given me.*

Rahner knew that he was a pilgrim toward God, ultimately at the mercy of the realities he could in the end only hint at. What was almost his final public sentence (for he was to die very soon afterward) may be simple and pious when much of his writing and lecturing had been convoluted and critical. But it nevertheless typifies the spirit in which Rahner offered all his work. It was no bad way to end.

Bibliography

"Die Jesuiten und die Zukunft: Anläßlich eines historischen Datums," *Frankfurter Allgemeine Zeitung,* August 31, 1973.

The Dynamic Element in the Church. Translated by W. J. O'Hara. London: Burns and Oates, 1964. *Das dynamische in der Kirche.* Freiburg: Herder, 1958.

Encounters with Silence (1937). Translated by James M. Demske. Westminster, Md.: Newman Press, 1966 [1960]. *Worte ins Schweigen.* Innsbruck: Rauch, 1938.

Everyday Things. Translated by M. H. Heelan. London: Sheed and Ward, 1965. *Alltägliche Dinge.* Einsiedeln: Benziger, 1964.

"Experiences of a Catholic Theologian" (1984). Translated by Declan Marmion and Gesa Thiessen. *Theological Studies* 61 (2000): 3–15. "Erfahrungen eines katholischen Theologen," in *Karl Rahner in Erinnerung.* Edited by Albert Raffelt. Düsseldorf: Patmos, 1994. 134–48.

Foundations of Christian Faith: An Introduction to the Idea of Christianity. Translated by William V. Dych. London: Darton, Longman and Todd, 1978. *Grundkurs des Glaubens: Einführung in den Begriff des Christentums.* Freiburg: Herder, 1976.

"Homily for the Feast of St. Stanislaus" (1942?), Karl-Rahner Archiv, 1.C.48.

Horizonte der Religiosität. Edited by Georg Sporschill. Vienna: Herold, 1984.

"Ignatius of Loyola Speaks to a Modern Jesuit" (1978). In *Ignatius of Loyola.* Translated by Rosaleen Ockenden. London: Collins, 1979. "Rede des Ignatius von Loyola an einen Jesuiten von heute." In *Schriften zur Theologie,* vol. 15. Einsiedeln: Benziger, 1983, 373–408.

Is Christian Life Possible Today?: Questions and Answers on the Fundamentals of Christian Life. Translated by Salvator Attanasio. Denville, N.J.: Dimension Books, 1984. *Mein Problem: Karl Rahner antwortet jungen Menschen.* Freiburg: Herder, 1982.

Mary, Mother of the Lord (1954), translated by W. J. O'Hara. Wheathampstead, U.K.: Antony Clarke, 1974 [1963]. *Maria, Mutter des Herrn* (Freiburg: Herder, 1956).

Meditations on Priestly Life (1961). Translated by Edward Quinn. London: Sheed and Ward, 1970. *Einübung Priestlicher Existenz.* Freiburg: Herder, 1973.

The Need and the Blessing of Prayer (1946). Translated by Bruce W. Gillette. 1946. Collegeville, Minn.: Liturgical Press, 1997. An earlier paraphrase was published in Ireland under the title of *Happiness through Prayer. Von der Not und dem Segen des Gebetes,* 4th edition. Innsbruck: Rauch, 1949.

Prayers of a Lifetime. Edited by Albert Raffelt. Edinburgh: T. & T. Clark, 1986. *Gebete des Lebens.* Freiburg: Herder, 1984.

Sehnsucht nach dem geheimnisvollen Gott: Profil–Bilder–Texte. Edited by Herbert Vorgrimler. Freiburg: Herder, 1990.

Servants of the Lord. Translated by Richard Strachan. New York: Herder and Herder, 1968. *Knechte Christi.* Freiburg: Herder, 1967.

Spiritual Exercises (1954–55). Translated by Kenneth Baker. London: Sheed and Ward, 1967. *Betrachtungen zum Ignatianischen Exerzitienbuch.* Munich: Kösel, 1965.

Theological Investigations. 23 vols. Translated by various hands. London: Darton, Longman and Todd, and New York: Crossroad, 1961–92. *Schriften zur Theologie.* 16 vols. Einsiedeln: Benziger, 1954–83.

Theology of Pastoral Action. Translated by W. J. O'Hara and adapted by Daniel Morrissey. New York: Herder, 1968. Chapters from volume 1.2. of *Handbuch der Pastoraltheologie.* Freiburg: Herder, 1964.